One More Strain of Praise

Sing we now at part - ing One more strain of praise.

To our Heav'n-ly Fa - ther Sweet - est songs we'll raise.

For his lov - ing kind - ness, For his ten - der care,

Let our songs of glad - ness Fill this Sab-bath air.

One More Strain of Praise

Neal A. Maxwell

Bookcraft

Salt Lake City, Utah

Copyright © 1999 by Bookcraft, Inc.

Library of Congress Catalog Card Number: 99-73569

ISBN 1-57008-679-6

First Printing, 1999

Printed in the United States of America

Sing We Now at Parting

Sing we now at parting
One more strain of praise.
To our Heav'nly Father
Sweetest songs we'll raise.
For his loving kindness,
For his tender care,
Let our songs of gladness
Fill this Sabbath air.

Praise him for his mercy;
Praise him for his love.
For unnumbered blessings
Praise the Lord above.
Let our happy voices
Still the notes prolong.
One alone is worthy
Of our sweetest song.

Jesus, our Redeemer,
Now our praises hear.
While we bow before thee,
Lend a list'ning ear.
Save us, Lord, from error.
Watch us day by day.
Help us now to serve thee
In a pleasing way.

—George Manwaring

Contents

Introduction

Many have helped me much with my illness. This is especially true of my oncologist, Dr. Clyde Ford, who has walked with me down the path of leukemia, including both his medical and his personal part in providing the blessed "delay en route."

Given all the "IV's" and literally hundreds of necessary injections to maintain and facilitate the "delay," this seems to be my life's pincushion period. Dr. Larry Staker, my primary-care physician, has been attentive and helpful both during and before these last leukemic years. Dr. David Hill did "house calls" when my sinus problems caused concern from time to time. Numerous nurses have helped me greatly, especially Cara Mickelsen, Michelle Tittensor, Heather Swain, Julie McCandless, but also unnamed others.

All these individuals did not merely go through the motions but also went sensitively through the emotions—of mine as well as other patients' illnesses—maximizing what medicine can contribute when combined with kind care.

It is unsurprising that my wife, Colleen, has been the most responsive and helpful. This has included many times when her own supply of energy was low. Yet she was ever anxious not only to care for me but also to please me, and even to surprise me in different and thoughtful ways.

Our children and their spouses (Becky and Mike, Cory and Karen, Nancy and Mark, Jane and Marc) and all the grandchildren have likewise been special. Some may say that such familial love is merely to be expected, and in one sense it is. But when people do their family duties well, the rest of us are obvious beneficiaries. Then, rather than being something one takes for granted, it is something so generously granted in which one rejoices.

Not only have Colleen and the family, including my extended family, been superb, but Susan Jackson has also been a secondary sufferer, while being a primary helper. Furthermore, the regular prayers of so many members and friends in so many places have blessed and nurtured me, and still do, for which I shall be everlastingly grateful.

Finally, if more than in my past writings this spare volume blends the autobiographical and the doctrinal, it is because these two dimensions are actually inseparable, for I am long since rooted in the restored doctrines of the kingdom, however imperfectly I reflect them.

Doctrines believed and practiced do change and improve us, while ensuring our vital access to the Spirit. Both outcomes are crucial. No wonder, therefore, *One More Strain of Praise* especially for Jesus Christ (with chapter titles taken from the same hymn) focuses on certain key doctrines, because these continue to pervade my personal discipleship and help me to press forward in the great distance yet to be covered as to my personal improvement. How could it be otherwise? The scriptures, which we are to "liken unto ourselves," inevitably and blessedly blend the autobiographical with the doctrinal. (See 1 Nephi 19:23.)

I alone am responsible for the contents of this book, which, of course, is not an official Church publication, though I sincerely hope it will be helpful to the readers.

■

CHAPTER ONE

"Still the Notes Prolong"

Why is it that I couldn't see the illness coming? Looking back, I now recognize there were more than a few pointing indicators in addition to unusual fatigue. For instance, there was the operative role of irony about which, for years, I have spoken and written. But now it was my turn to experience it more keenly. The very title of my latest book was almost invitational—*If Thou Endure It Well*. This by itself might have alerted me, being issued just before the leukemia was diagnosed. Consider, as well, the book's ending poem, which was more invitational than poetic:

SUBMISSION
By Neal A. Maxwell

When from Thy stern tutoring
I would quickly flee,
Turn me from my Tarshish
To where is best for me.

Help me in my Nineveh
To serve with love and truth—
Not on a hillside posted
Mid shade of gourd or booth.

When my modest suffering seems
So vexing, wrong, and sore,
May I recall what freely flowed
From each and every pore.

Dear Lord of the Abba Cry,
Help me in my duress
To endure it well enough
And to say, . . . "Nevertheless."

Irony, the hard crust on the bread of adversity, can try both our faith and our patience (see Mosiah 23:21). Irony can be a particularly pointed form of such chastening, because it involves disturbing incongruity, contrary to our expectations. Our best-laid and even worthy plans must be sharply revised.

With such an inverting of our anticipated consequences, irony can become the frequent cause of an individual's being offended. Furthermore, the larger and the more untamed one's ego, the greater the likelihood of his being offended, especially when tasting his small portion of vinegar and gall.

It was ironic, too, that an Emily Dickinson poem was used in that same precursor book. This could have been another personal "heads up."

He stuns you by degrees—
Prepares your brittle Nature
For the Etherial Blow
By fainter Hammers—further heard—
Then nearer—Then so slow
Your Breath has time to straighten—
Your Brain—to bubble Cool—
Deals—One—imperial—Thunderbolt—
That scalps your naked Soul—

(From poem 315, *The Poems of Emily Dickinson,* ed. Thomas H. Johnson [Cambridge, Mass.: The Belknap Press of Harvard University Press, 1955], p. 238.)

Likewise, a 1995 Thanksgiving talk constituted something of a "pass in review," utilizing for the first time a previously resisted autobiographical approach. The focus was on a few special examples of my gratitude to God for the various intertwinings of my life with the lives of others.

Also emblematic and foretelling was another crescendo of sorts during my assignment in the late spring of 1995 to the Okinawa Stake conference. This visit coincided with the fiftieth anniversary of the end of the World War II fighting on that island, where I was an eighteen-year-old, inadequate, and frightened infantryman. The commemorative visit stirred many memories and much gratitude, as it doubtless did in several hundred other veterans returning to that island.

Subsequently, too, several small luncheon gatherings of surviving Okinawa and World War II buddies back home tied other needed loops together. This tying together, too, could have signaled what was impending. Those buddies, along with many members and nonmembers alike, have been enclosing me in an enveloping pattern of prayers and concern.

Interviews about my faith by an able Hugh Hewitt on PBS in 1996 also turned out to be significantly autobiographical. This focus was not needed by viewers as much as by me—at least for the purpose of counting my blessings.

Beginning in January 1997, chemotherapy treatment and hospitalization lasted forty-six days. My preceding desires were strong and settled but without knowing whether there was to be a remission of my leukemia at all. These desires included:

1. To be able to partake of this, my comparatively small-scale experience, and yet "not shrink" (see D&C 19:18).

2. To learn still more of Jesus by taking upon me a very small version of His yoke, and, in so doing, advancing my desire to become much more like Him (Matthew 11:29).

3. To increase my empathy so that I could also be more helpful to others, while at the same time being more effectively expressive of my ever-deepening convictions about the Savior and His gospel.

4. To follow the dictum of Brigham Young about how members of the Church (whether in persecution, poverty, or sickness, and so on) should acknowledge the hand of the Lord by saying, in effect, "It's all right":

When the Latter-day Saints make up their minds to endure, for the kingdom of God's sake, whatsoever shall come, whether poverty or riches, whether sickness or to be driven by mobs, they will say *it is all right*, and will honor the hand of the Lord in it, and in all things, and serve Him to the end of their lives, according to the best of their ability, God being their helper. If you have not made up your minds for this, the quicker you do so the better. (In *Journal of Discourses* 1:338; emphasis added.)

These same goals continued with me in the additional "IV" and injection chemotherapies of 1997, 1998, and 1999.

Amid it all, by giving further praise of the Master, I hope it will be said that I could "still the notes prolong."

Yes, my seventy-plus years surely constitute a generous span. But still, generous spans even with added delays en route "glide swiftly away":

> Our life as a dream,
> our time as a stream
> Glide swiftly away, . . .
> For the arrow is flown
> and the moments are gone.
>
> (Charles Wesley, "Come, Let Us Anew,"
> *Hymns*, no. 217.)

The test for all of us is how well we do within our individualized fields of action and in "those years wherein we are set," just as Tolkien wrote:

> Other evils there are that may come. . . . Yet it is not
> our part to master all the tides of the world, but to do what
> is in us for the succour of those years wherein we are set,

uprooting the evil in the fields that we know, so that those who live after may have clean earth to till. What weather they shall have is not ours to rule. (Gandalf in J. R. R. Tolkien, *The Return of the King* [New York: Ballantine Books, 1965], p. 190.)

A few brave disciples, in rare circumstances, are permitted to seal their testimonies with their blood. All of us, however, can witness, though less dramatically, by both how well we live and how well we die. By enduring well any deprivations and sufferings we can quietly but firmly seal our testimonies using the wax in our spiritual submissiveness.

As to how essential such submissiveness is, Gilbert Meilaender appropriately reminded us recently that C. S. Lewis, in *The Pilgrim's Regress*, spoke of how developmental discipleship always involves the "tether and pang of the particular." Concluding of Lewis's insights, Meilaender wrote: "We live with this duality of our being, with our hearts both tied to what is local and unique and drawn toward the universal. Living within that tension, as the Lewis poem puts it, 'we pay dearly.'" ("The Everyday C. S. Lewis," *First Things*, August/September 1998, p. 31.)

Yet my cross is comparatively light even now. It is surely less rough-hewn, compared to so many heavier crosses borne longer by others. Of course, only Jesus can accurately compare crosses. But whatever the ruggedness and weight, His grace is sufficient to help each of us carry his own cross (2 Corinthians 12:9; see also Ether 12:26-27; Moroni 10:32; D&C 17:8). Furthermore, whatever the weight of these tutorial challenges, if we emulate Job we won't "charge God foolishly" either (Job 1:22).

Among the lessons learned and, yes, re-learned, for which praise of the Master is surely given, were the following:

- Suffering accounts for some of the sweat that goes with the process of working out our salvation.

- Customized tutorials are the extra tuition we pay for our continuing, graduate education as Jesus' disciples.

- Some blessings clearly come in the form of bracings. Therefore, both recesses and brief reveries are of necessity quickly interrupted because of life's compressed curriculum.

- Since smugness stifles the process of spiritual growth, smugness is likely to be shattered, too, and not just arrogance, an obvious candidate for shattering. More especially, bracings can interrupt any tendency to be gliding along, like a hydrofoil, too unfeeling of and unresponsive to the shaping bumps and waves of the sea of life.

- It is best if we can be humble because of the word and not solely because circumstances compel us to be humble, but, if necessary, the latter will do.

- In discipleship, we learn of suffering that there are no exemptions, only variations.

- We continue to feel that we would still prefer to suffer ourselves rather than to see our children or grandchildren suffer. Yet this choice is sometimes not given to us.

- We learn that we can "take" more than we first imagined, yet we fervently hope such a response will also prove true of how we handle any encores.

- We learn much more about the Holy Ghost's role as the Comforter, including how He so helpfully preaches to us from the pulpit of memory in order to help us cope with our present and future.

- We learn that, while others can sincerely comfort and help us, even so, our cross is finally ours alone to bear.

- Prayers, after all, are the most effective thing others can do for us! These constitute an outpouring that, for me, has become and continues to be such a real and sustaining factor.

- Heavenly Father not only expects but also encourages us to plead with Him over our challenges. Our pleading is not a sign of weakness, but can reflect thoughtful submissiveness. Indeed, Jesus, who knew clearly what He faced in Gethsemane and on Calvary, nevertheless pleaded with the Lord for the cup to be removed from Him. Therefore it is what we do, during and after the pleading, that matters, especially as to our submissiveness to the Lord. But pleadings are appropriate.

I feel unworthy of the many incoming prayers, letters, and phone calls, yet surely not unappreciative! Being thus remembered by so many is truly an overwhelming experience; one simply cannot imagine, beforehand, the real metes and bounds or the deep tenderness and gratitude that this outreach by others evokes.

Clearly there are different individual exit routes from life. Some people go suddenly and quickly, leaving survivors in a state of shock and with almost no time to prepare. Others die only after prolonged suffering. It is best that we leave to the Lord the variations in both the timing and the exit routes. He and He alone can make those decisions, and He does so out of His individualized perfect love and mercy.

Thanks to Jesus, however, whether we go suddenly and easily or agonizingly and slowly, His glorious latter-day Restoration is part of His helping grace, being so full of nurturing doctrines and reassuring truths. The fundamental purposes of the Restoration included "to bear testimony of mine Only Begotten; his resurrection from the dead; yea, and also the resurrection of all men," two supernal fundamentals (Moses 7:62). Other restored realities are clearly a vital part of the grace of it all, but Jesus' atonement and the resurrection are at the very center of it all.

By means of the resplendent and reassuring Restoration, so many other things that constitute the "tether and pang of the particular" can be put in a proper perspective. Praise be to God, because the gospel permits us to see even more clearly "things as they really are, and . . . things as they really will be" (Jacob 4:13). If things are not seen with such gospel clarity, so many mortal lives end up being consumed by such puny purposes. Otherwise, too, without gospel perspectives human capacity can be so underemployed and improperly focused, like trying to use the huge telescope on Mt. Palomar merely to study nearby Catalina Island. The grand *Restoration* is not only a crucial and needed *restitution* of "plain and precious things" but it is also a *refutation* of various prevailing and incorrect views of life, including the view that life is merely a meaningless brevity.

Therefore, matching life's strategic purposes to our local discipleship and its daily tasks by using gospel perspectives becomes vital. In this process, adversity can both clean the lens and sharpen life's focus while blending the doctrinal and the personal.

Father's plan comprehends and is inlaid with His personal plans for each of us, including our individual trajectories of trial. Happily, therefore, we can rightly sing in praise and of exemplifying Jesus:

> He marked the path and led the way,
> And ev'ry point defines . . .
> Redemption's grand design,
> Where justice, love, and mercy meet
> In harmony divine!
>
> (Eliza R. Snow, "How Great the Wisdom
> and the Love," *Hymns*, no. 195.)

Thus recent events in my life have helped me to try more valiantly to "prolong" these and other grateful notes of praise for the Lord, since these are part of the music of discipleship.

Besides, our shared uncertainty as to proximate things simply goes with the mortal territory. Only a few people seem to have known something of their longevity and personal timetables. The Prophet Joseph Smith knew his life would not be a long one and that he would never see forty. President Brigham Young, who visited Joseph in Liberty Jail, said, "I heard Joseph say many a time, 'I shall not live until I am forty years of age'" (*Discourses of Brigham Young*, sel. John A. Widtsoe [Salt Lake City: Deseret Book Co., 1941], p. 467). President Wilford Woodruff's journal records that Lyman Wight "said that Joseph told him, while in Liberty jail, Missouri, in 1839, he would not live to see forty years" (*History of the Church* 7:212). Most of us do not know our spans. Nevertheless, though these are unrevealed, "all things must come to pass in their time" (D&C 64:32).

Therefore, as to our personal timing, the rest of us are asked to live in what someone has called "cheerful insecurity." We trust in the timing of the Lord, and, meanwhile, know that the days and years of righteous individuals will not be numbered less. But it is up to us "to be content with the things which the Lord hath allotted unto [us]," including the time allotted (Alma 29:3-4).

Meanwhile, we surely experience the varied but real limitations in the ranges of our "tether" and the customized "pang" of our "particular" and allotted challenges (see Alma 29). Meanwhile, too, we experience the reality that there are different types of tears: tears of sheer joy; tears of sadness, including over those who suffer because of sin or who have no hope for a glorious resurrection. But there are also the tears that are shed out of sheer empathy, as when tenderness responds to tenderness and empathy evokes empathy. Such occurred in the case of the death of Lazarus. Jesus did not go at once, as requested, to bless sick Lazarus, but instead arrived only after Lazarus had died. (See John chapters 11 and 12.) Jesus knew beforehand, of course, that Lazarus would rise again; He knew the impending outcome. But even so, when upon His arrival He saw the tears of faith-filled Mary and others, Jesus nevertheless wept. Yes, He surely loved Lazarus. Yes, He was about to raise him dramatically from the grave. Yet seeing the tears of others evoked His own empathic tears.

Such reciprocal evocations have been part of my experience many times in recent months. Empathic tears, therefore, do not reflect a fear of death, but instead a precious sharing of emotions, as when others are touched and are so kindly expressive to us.

In any case, uncertainty as to longevity leaves a balance to be struck by us all. We are to salute the Lord for the gift of life, for as long as it lasts, and yet, at the same time, to be spiritually submissive as it ends. This is a delicate balance we do not always fully and gracefully achieve.

Several scriptures have proved to be relevant and reassuring in this regard. When these have been shared aloud with many who also suffer from cancer they have been far better than anything I could say, especially to those valiants who reach that point where they are sick of being sick.

> And I said unto him: I know that [God] loveth his children; nevertheless, I do not know the meaning of all things (1 Nephi 11:17).

We need not "know the meaning of all things," if we know God loves us! In the same way our appreciativeness for the role of submissiveness needs to grow, as one strives to [become] a saint through the atonement of Christ the Lord, and [become] as a child, submissive, meek, humble, patient, full of love, willing to submit to all things which the Lord seeth fit to inflict upon him, even as a child doth submit to his father (Mosiah 3:19).

Use of the word *inflict* suggests customized challenges and tutoring that require an added and special submissiveness.

Similarly, our appreciativeness of Jesus' supernal empathy will greatly help us to endure.

And he shall go forth, suffering pains and afflictions and temptations of every kind; and this that the word might be fulfilled which saith he will take upon him the pains and the sicknesses of his people.

And he will take upon him death, that he may loose the bands of death which bind his people; and he will take upon him their infirmities, that his bowels may be filled with mercy, according to the flesh, that he may know according to the flesh how to succor his people according to their infirmities. (Alma 7:11-12.)

Jesus fully understands! His empathy is perfect!

No wonder it is intellectually dishonest not to inventory all of one's blessings great and small. No wonder there is a reminding scriptural theme all about how God has mercifully blessed mankind—and for such a long time:

Behold, I would exhort you that when ye shall read these things, if it be wisdom in God that ye should read them, that ye would remember how merciful the Lord hath been unto the children of men, from the creation of Adam even down until the time that ye shall receive these things, and ponder it in your hearts (Moroni 10:3).

The vast sweep of divine oversight of human history includes God's many mercies to us individually. Of course, when death comes to all of us, as a result thereof some things will be clearly missed. But these are small dunes of deprivation when placed alongside that vast Himalayan range of all our past and present blessings.

It is significant that the very first verse in the Book of Mormon reflects Nephi's own experiential gratitude for the goodness of God. "Having seen many afflictions in the course of my days, nevertheless [I was] highly favored of the Lord in all my days." Yet, he continued, he had a "great knowledge of the goodness . . . of God." This knowledge was something on which Nephi repeatedly relied during his life to sustain him through so much adversity. (See 1 Nephi 1:1.)

Even so, unless we are on guard it is easy to slip quickly into self-pity. For me, however, there was the helpfulness of those who have gone before, including my parents, who have modeled so well for me the process of dying.

In any case, the "delay en route" granted me has been a special blessing for which I praise God, and I have been reasonably busy trying to use the allotted mortal time for the purposes of eternity.

So now, as in my past efforts to write about discipleship, I give prime attention to doctrinal matters and to gospel principles. These informing and emancipating elements are crucial in order for us all to function within the "tethers and pangs" of our individual lives and times.

So many doctrines could have been selected and illustrated. Those to follow—being of good cheer, Jesus' redemptive role as our advocate, God's mercy, the need for personal purification, the blessings and challenges of moral agency, and the counting of my blessings—all these have a poignancy and relevancy for this sunset period of my discipleship.

Having ultimate gospel "gladness," therefore, not only is possible but also can finally, if not constantly, swallow up any proximate sadness. Thus the music of faith not only deserves to be prolonged but also should include lively "songs of gladness" such as those that follow.

CHAPTER TWO

"Songs of Gladness"

In exulting over the gloriousness and expansiveness of the Restoration, the much-persecuted Prophet Joseph Smith exclaimed, "Shall we not go on in so great a cause?" (D&C 128:22.) The gospel's "gladness" actually is so enlivening. It can help us to be of good cheer in a time when other things could dominate, globally and personally, with their dampening pervasiveness. God is deserving of our praise for providing us with much-needed precious perspective. Of necessity there are sunsets in our individual lives, yet so far as gospel perspectives are concerned it is always "the morning breaks" (*Hymns*, no. 1). This light grows ever "brighter until the perfect day" (D&C 50:24).

In such a climactic time as the last days, we shall see things both wonderful and awful. Joel and Zephaniah prophesied that the last times would be a "day of . . . gloominess" (Joel 2:2; Zephaniah 1:15). Even so, this is all the more reason for us to "shine as lights in the world" (Philippians 2:15). So illuminated, we can better help to gather the Lord's flock in the last days from wherever they have been scattered in the "cloudy and dark day" (Ezekiel 34:12; see also 30:3).

Yet even as some things clearly worsen in the world, the true Saints will simply get better. Furthermore, letting our lights shine includes a measure of wise public and community service by doing what we can do to better our small portion of the world. We of all people can thus be, to borrow a phrase, "idealists without illusions" by contributing to and by being "anxiously engaged" in good causes.

Gloom and despair will nevertheless grow almost ratio-like, because "despair cometh because of iniquity" (Moroni 10:22). Consider this latter-day overlay foreseen by President Brigham Young:

> It was revealed to me in the commencement of this Church, that the Church would spread, prosper, grow and extend, and that in proportion to the spread of the Gospel among the nations of the earth, so would the power of Satan rise (in *Journal of Discourses* 13:280).

Hence there is no way that we and our posterity can be a part of the last days and expect overall conditions to be otherwise. Such despair will inexorably accelerate the various ways in which "love . . . shall wax cold" (Matthew 24:12).

Likewise accelerating the latter-day developments is our heightened collective awareness of the global human condition, an awareness now made possible by unprecedented technology. Technology brings an almost daily awareness of global inhumanities and tragedies that were once remote. Consider, for instance, the highly different "coverage" given at the time to two dissimilar but shaping conflicts: The battle of Waterloo and the Gulf War. (Not just the delay in reporting Waterloo versus the immediacy of the Gulf War, but mere paper and word of mouth versus graphic films and television viewed by millions.)

Just what is the human capacity today for absorbing such a steady flow of gloomy and tragic news? We do not know, but the impact is real, and it can add subtly and directly to the despair. Nevertheless, will we still sincerely sing songs of individual gladness amid such gloom?

President Joseph F. Smith wisely counseled:

The leaders of the people should never disseminate a spirit of gloom in the hearts of the people. If men standing in high places sometimes feel the weight and anxiety of momentous times, they should be all the firmer and all the more resolute in those convictions which come from a God-fearing conscience and pure lives. . . . It is a matter of the greatest importance that the people be educated to appreciate and cultivate the bright side of life rather than to permit its darkness and shadows to hover over them. (*Gospel Doctrine* [Salt Lake City: Deseret Book Co., 1939], p. 155.)

Thus Jesus, the greatest leader of all, in spite of the most ominous challenges He faced, consistently admonished His disciples to "be of good cheer" (Matthew 14:27).

Another way is to lighten the load and do what Paul noted: "that ye have put off the old man with his deeds" (Colossians 3:9). King Benjamin preceded what was later preserved from Paul by elaborating:

For the natural man is an enemy to God, and has been from the fall of Adam, and will be, forever and ever, unless he yields to the enticings of the Holy Spirit, and putteth off the natural man and becometh a saint through the atonement of Christ the Lord, and becometh as a child, submissive, meek, humble, patient, full of love, willing to submit to all things which the Lord seeth fit to inflict upon him, even as a child doth submit to his father (Mosiah 3:19).

Brigham Young, a careful student of the Book of Mormon, was likewise quick to see and to use the same metaphor in his teachings concerning "the natural man":

How difficult it is to teach the natural man, who comprehends nothing more than that which he sees with the natural eye! . . . Talk to him about angels, heavens, God, immortality, and eternal lives, and it is like sounding brass, or a tinkling cymbal to his ears; it has no music to him; there is nothing in it that charms his senses, soothes his feelings, attracts his attention, or engages his affections, in the least. (*Discourses of Brigham Young*, sel. John A. Widtsoe [Salt Lake City: Deseret Book Co., 1941], p. 260.)

Brigham thus understood, as did Paul, how to the natural man the things of the Spirit "are foolishness" (1 Corinthians 2:14).

Even given our challenging context, however, we are instructed by our Lord and Exemplar, Jesus Christ, to "be of good cheer" (D&C 61:36; 78:18). How can this be achieved?

For one thing, discernment is vital. The eminent historian Will Durant wrote of the human need for perspective and proportion in order "to know that the little things are little, and the big things big, before it is too late; we want to see things now as they will seem forever—'in the light of eternity'" (*The Story of Philosophy* [New York: Simon and Schuster, 1927], p. 1).

Scriptural illustrations are especially instructive. Jesus told the original Twelve to be of good cheer when at that time, on the roiling surface of circumstance, there was nothing to be cheerful about. How could Jesus expect the Twelve to be of good cheer? Because, the Savior explained, "in the world ye shall have tribulation: but be of good cheer; I have overcome the world." (John 16:33.) His impending triumph was to become the central fact of human history!

Thus it is vital that we not let grim prophecies "weigh [us] down," but, rather, we are to let Christ and all He accomplished lift us up. This will occur if the Atonement "[rests] in [our minds] forever," said Mormon in his counsel to Moroni amid their own very difficult conditions back then. (Moroni 9:25.)

The reasons for "good cheer" are strategic, therefore, whereas life's vexations, though real, are actually tactical. This distinction between the strategic and the tactical is enormously important for us to understand, lest the daily drumbeat of the tactical "weigh" us down. Of course, discipleship is focused instead on the ultimate "there and then," on the glorious and eternal things. But the daily "here and now" vexations and challenges are nevertheless so specific.

For the original Twelve, therefore, it was crucial to

know these grand facts: Christ had overcome the world; the Atonement was about to be accomplished; death would be irrevocably defeated; and all mankind would be given—through the grace of God—immortality! Satan, with all his sound and fury, had failed to prevent the accomplishment of the centerpiece in the plan of salvation! And for those of deep faith, because of the same emancipating atonement, there would be the added richness of God's greatest gift, eternal life! (D&C 6:13; 14:7.) Immortality *plus!*

These resplendent realities and fundamental facts thus justified the Twelve's being of good cheer. Never mind their grim, temporary circumstances, including how the Mortal Messiah's disheartened followers would be temporarily scattered like sheep (Matthew 26:31).

If inventoried, Jesus' urgings regarding good cheer are always connected with, lead to, or illustrate transcending things. For instance, Jesus told one individual to be of good cheer because his sins had been forgiven (Matthew 9:2). What good news! Again, gospel proportion can help us to be of good cheer, especially about things that matter.

The same words, "be of good cheer," were used when the disciples were terrified as they saw Jesus walking on the stormy waters of Galilee. This dramatic demonstration of Christ's divinity was one of many, but the summary words, "Be of good cheer; it is I," surely evoked a grateful and reassuring response then (Matthew 14:27). Moreover, how often must this memory and these words have evoked special and nurturing memories in the times that followed Jesus' ascension?

To latter-day disciples in the midst of tribulation, Christ has urged that we be of good cheer, "for I will lead you along" (D&C 78:18). Anciently, Enoch's joy came about over similar reassuring fundamental facts. Speaking of the Lord, Enoch exclaimed reassuringly, "Yet thou art there" (Moses 7:30). One's current, local context is undeniably significant, but the Lord's purposes will finally triumph, for He is surely "there."

Of pleading Enoch, Hugh Nibley wrote:

> Enoch is the great advocate, the champion of the human race, pleading with God to spare the wicked and "refusing to be comforted" until he is shown just how that is to be done. He feels for all and is concerned for all. He is the passionate and compassionate, the magnanimous one who cannot rest knowing that others are miserable. He is the wise and obedient servant, the friend and helper of all, hence the perfect leader and ruler. (*Enoch the Prophet,* vol. 2 of *The Collected Works of Hugh Nibley* [Salt Lake City and Provo, Utah: Deseret Book Co. and Foundation for Ancient Research and Mormon Studies, 1986], p. 21.)

Though Enoch was permitted to see the human misery caused by human wickedness in Noah's time and "refused to be comforted" (Moses 7:44), what finally comforted him were the revelations and the assurances given to him about Jesus' role as Redeemer and the eventual Restoration in the latter days.

The same fundamentals can comfort us even when our tactical situations may be grim, providing us with gospel gladness even amid momentary sadness. Hence, the pressing and vexing things of the moment should not be allowed to obscure the later things of eternity, "things as they really will be" (Jacob 4:13).

The trouble is that, unless careful, we still tend to let some obscuring occur, don't we? It is only through our own Spirit-led experience that we can come to savor the distinction between the things of eternity and the things of the moment. The things of the moment can be so real and intense. In fact, they are designed to get our attention!

This same precious perspective was needed on another occasion when at night the resurrected Jesus stood by an imprisoned Paul, instructing Paul to be of good cheer (Acts 23:11). Once again, the circumstances of the moment hardly favored cheer. They included Paul's having been humiliatingly and publicly struck on the mouth by order of Ananias, the high priest. Forty individuals were plotting Paul's death. He faced a trial for sedition. Why, therefore, should he be of good cheer? Because, Jesus announced, Paul, though then in depressing circumstances, would soon take the "glad tidings," the good news of the gospel, to Rome! Never mind either that martyrdom also awaited Paul there.

Church members in another age were held as virtual hostages until certain prophecies were fulfilled. Their lives would be forfeited if those prophecies about Jesus' birth were not fulfilled precisely on time. (3 Nephi 1:5-13.) They were nevertheless told by the Lord to be of good cheer. Why? Because, said Jesus, "on the morrow come I into the world" (3 Nephi 1:13). With His birth, "on the morrow," the mortal ministry of the Messiah would, at last, begin, and the emancipating atonement would be soon achieved. Therefore, what were a mere thirty or so additional years, when some had awaited the resurrection for centuries?

Even so, in the midst of "all these things [which] give [us] experience," do we sometimes get discouraged? Of course! Consider how in the late 1820s Brigham Young, as yet untouched by the restored gospel, was apparently a somewhat discouraged young man. He found himself disapproving of much of what he saw in the world, and he wondered whether he had a work to do. His loving brother, Phineas, gave Brigham prescient, personal counsel: "Hang on, for I know the Lord is agoing to do some thing for us." (Sermon of Heber C. Kimball, in Minutes, 8 January 1845, Brigham Young Papers, Archives Division, Church Historical Department, The Church of Jesus Christ of Latter-day Saints, Salt Lake City, Utah.) What later happened is Moses-like history.

We, too, can "hang on" when we know who we are, and when we trust God's purposes. We, too, can truly be trusting and be of good cheer even when the swirling circumstances of the moment still toss us about.

Therefore we should not let murmuring—even clever murmuring—undercut good cheer by our half-suppressed resentments or muttered complaints. We all remember in *Fiddler on the Roof* Tevye's verbal asides to God. Since the ultimate "Addressee" of some of our murmuring is clearly the Lord, as when the people complained against Moses, at least Tevye honestly acknowledged to Whom he addressed his complaints. (See Exodus 16:8; 1 Nephi 16:20.)

Instead of gladness, murmuring seems to come so naturally to the natural man. It crosses the spectrum of complaints. We need bread. We need water. (See Numbers 21:5.) The needed military reinforcements did not arrive (see Alma 60). "Why did we ever leave Egypt?" (See Numbers 11:20.) "Why did we ever leave Jerusalem?" (See 1 Nephi 2:11.) On and on goes our murmuring, and, it is significant that it almost always focuses on our tactical frustrations.

One underlying and fundamental fact best explains our failing to be of good cheer: "And thus Laman and Lemuel . . . did murmur because they knew not the dealings of that God who had created them" (1 Nephi 2:12). Like Laman and Lemuel, we too sometimes fail to understand the dealings of our God in our lives and in our times. (See also 1 Nephi 17:22.)

Too many of us seem to expect that life will flow ever smoothly, featuring an unbroken chain of green lights with empty parking places just in front of our destinations.

In its extremity, despair not only reflects immediate discontentment but also incorporates feelings of very deep ambivalence and/or confusion about the nature of life: "Their sorrowing was . . . the sorrowing of the damned, because [they could not] take happiness in sin" (see Mormon 2:13, 14).

By knowing that the everlasting and ultimate things are firmly in place, can we not then better endure irritations such as a dislocated travel schedule? Besides, how can it rain on the just and the unjust alike without occasionally raining on our personal parades? (See Matthew 5:45.)

Knowing who we are surely helps, along with knowing about the "dealings" of God with His children (1 Nephi 2:12; 17:22).

In the midst of this mortal experience we will even see the unrighteous succeed—at least temporarily and in worldly terms. On occasion we might be tempted to complain, as some did anciently, that the wicked seem to get away with it (see Malachi 3).

Such conditions in our days thus call for spiritual spunk in each of us. Spiritual spunk can actually break up frustrating stumbling blocks, turning them into stepping stones, just as weaknesses can be transformed into strengths (see Ether 12:27).

Besides, others are counting on us to be of good cheer. Otherwise, an irony can occur—one application of which Malcolm Muggeridge expressed as follows:

> I see it as one of the greatest ironies of this ironical time, that the Christian message should be withdrawn for consideration just when it is most desperately needed to save men's reason, if not their souls. It is as though a Salvation Army band, valiantly and patiently waiting through the long years for Judgment Day, should, when it comes at last, and the heavens do veritably begin to unfold like a scroll, throw away their instruments and flee in terror. (Quoted by William F. Buckley Jr., "Christianize Dartmouth?" *National Review*, March 23, 1998, p. 46.)

Remember how, momentarily, the disciples on a storm-tossed sea were frightened by their approaching Deliverer (see Matthew 14:22-36). Within this context of the opposites, cheer and despair, there is another ongoing and inner drama for all those who are serious disciples. From its personal effects we cannot be spared. Indeed, upon serious reflection we would not really wish to be spared from the divine discontent which is a necessary part of developing discipleship. This should not be confused, however, with the global gloom and despair previously noted.

This very process of spiritual isometrics commences when we rightly heed the beckoning call, "Yea, come unto Christ, and be perfected in him, and deny yourselves of all ungodliness" (Moroni 10:32). When we answer that call, something else happens, however, cheek-by-jowl: "And if men come unto me I will show unto them their weakness . . ." Then comes a special promise: "My grace is sufficient for all men that humble themselves before me; for if they humble themselves before me, and have faith in me, then will I make weak things become strong unto them." (Ether 12:27.)

This process is painful. It is unavoidable. It is repetitive. It is relentless! As to our repeated need to be taught one lesson all the time, Brigham Young observed:

> Men are organized to be independent in their sphere, . . . yet they have, as soldiers term it, to run the gauntlet all the time. . . . but that independency . . . must be proved and tried while in this state of existence, [it] must be operated upon by the good and the evil. (In *Journal of Discourses* 3:316.)

It is vital, therefore, for us to distinguish between, on the one hand, the growth pains inevitably felt during the process of discipleship and, on the other hand, the general, disoriented despair described earlier. Since the gospel lets us know the difference between proximate and ultimate things, we need not be confused. There can be proximate tribulation, but with ultimate salvation. There can be proximate disappointment but with ultimate joy. There can be local cloud cover but without general and lasting darkness!

Will we, therefore, have faith in God's hand—not only as to the grand plan of salvation but also in our specific, individual portion of the plan? In the midst of our troubles, trials, and afflictions will we trust in God that things will finally work out "all right"? Hence trusting is part of having faith in Him, in His plan, and in His timing, just as President Brigham Young conveyed, as noted earlier:

> When the Latter-day Saints make up their minds to endure, for the kingdom of God's sake, whatsoever shall come, whether poverty or riches, whether sickness or to be driven by mobs, they will say *it is all right*, and will honor the hand of the Lord in it, and in all things, and serve Him to the end of their lives (in *Journal of Discourses* 1:338; emphasis added).

The best way to acknowledge and confess God's hand is to reach out and take it. And so we should trust God as He works with us even in our weakness. "Nevertheless, the Lord God showeth us our weakness that we may know that it is by his grace, and his great condescensions unto the children of men, that we have power to do these things" (Jacob 4:7).

Being of good cheer, therefore, is a matter of spiritual perspective. Clearly it really takes faith. However, this faith must be fixed on "Jesus, our Redeemer," knowing, as we do, of His and the Father's perfections in all their attributes of character. They will not let us down—either now or "at the last day." (See Mosiah 23:22.) It is Their perfections that make genuine worship of Them possible, given the preeminence of the first commandment. Their ultimate character makes our proximate faith possible.

They are truly special, so we can gladly, as well as safely, praise Them!

This glorifying of God means that we should exult in and praise Him for His ultimate distinctiveness, worshiping Him without reservation or hesitation. The same reverence should flow to "Jesus, our Redeemer," for "there is none other name given whereby man can be saved" (D&C 18:23; 2 Nephi 25:20).

How awful the human predicament would be if They were really only a little better than we!

CHAPTER THREE

■

"Jesus, Our Redeemer"

Multiple revelations teach us that redeeming Jesus is uniquely our "advocate with the Father," that He pleads for us, and that He makes intercession for us (see 1 John 2:1; 2 Nephi 2:9; Mosiah 5:8; D&C 32:3; 45:3; 62:1; 110:4). Without this grand reality we would be helpless, and all would be truly and finally hopeless.

Jesus' personal role is unique in yet another way: "For the Father judgeth no man, but hath committed all judgment unto the Son" (John 5:22). "Jesus, our Redeemer," has earned this special standing, entitling Him not only to plead for us but also to judge us, which His unique suffering made possible by virtue of His agonies during the Atonement (see Mosiah 15:8; D&C 45:3–5). Thus, by His suffering and by divine investiture, in one sense Jesus is both advocate and judge!

Only an omniscient, all-loving God could have both roles of advocate (pleading for the petitioner) and judge (deciding the ultimate fate of the petitioner). This is because He possesses a perfect balance of the qualities of justice and mercy and all other divine attributes that make Him perfect, or complete, in all the Godly virtues.

First, to illustrate the unique role of Jesus as our Advocate, consider the following beautiful expression, using His very words, as He pleaded for the members of His infant, latter-day Church:

> Listen to him who is the advocate with the Father, who *is pleading* your cause before him—
>
> Saying: Father, behold the sufferings and death of him who did no sin, in whom thou wast well pleased; behold the blood of thy Son which was shed, the blood of him whom thou gavest that thyself might be glorified;
>
> Wherefore, Father, spare these my brethren that believe on my name, that they may come unto me and have everlasting life (D&C 45:3-5; emphasis added).

Thus what is very fundamental and doctrinal becomes very personal in its application. The satisfying of the requirements of divine justice by means of Jesus' great atonement is central to the Father's plan of salvation, a plan which clearly reflects and is sustained by Jesus' character and atonement, an atonement made possible by Jesus' character. In this happy and merciful situation, the Lord can forgive our sins, yet He "cannot look upon sin with the least degree of allowance," hence the unclean and unrepentant, though resurrected, will not be exalted (Alma 45:16; D&C 1:31).

> Now the work of justice could not be destroyed; if so, God would cease to be God.

And thus we see that all mankind were fallen, and they were in the grasp of justice; yea, the justice of God, which consigned them forever to be cut off from his presence. . . .

What, do ye suppose that mercy can rob justice? I say unto you, Nay; not one whit. If so, God would cease to be God. (Alma 42:13-14, 25; see also D&C 88:40.)

Even divine mercy cannot rob justice! Such, therefore, is the very basic need to satisfy the requirements of divine justice, which are "affixed," and thus "answer the ends of the atonement" (2 Nephi 2:10).

In God's plan of happiness the atoning Christ paid a debt He personally did not owe and at a costly price that we could not possibly pay by ourselves. Unlike the Father's plan, in today's context of indulgent secularism, however, too many insist that mercy "rob justice," and much more than "one whit." C. S. Lewis saw the modern trend coming well before it became more fully blown:

> The Humanitarian theory wants simply to abolish Justice and substitute Mercy for it. . . . Mercy, detached from Justice, grows unmerciful. That is the important paradox. As there are plants which flourish only in mountain soil, so it appears that Mercy will flower only when it grows in the crannies of the rock of Justice: transplanted to the marshlands of mere Humanitarianism, it becomes a man-eating weed, all the more dangerous because it is still called by the same name as the mountain variety. ("The Humanitarian Theory of Punishment" [1949], in *God in the Dock: Essays on Theology and Ethics*, ed. Walter Hooper [Grand Rapids, Mich.: Eerdmans, 1970], p. 294.)

Christ's atonement, first of all, blesses all mortals by conferring upon all of us the unearned gift of the universal resurrection: "For as in Adam all die, even so in Christ shall all be made alive" (1 Corinthians 15:22). Christ was thereby empowered by the Father to make intercession to authorize the resurrection for all: "And thus God breaketh the bands of death, having gained the victory over death; giving the Son power to make *intercession* for the children of men" (Mosiah 15:8; emphasis added).

As to the second and most glorious blessing flowing from the Atonement, however, namely eternal life, Christ's intercession is conditional: "If any man sin [AND REPENT], we have an *advocate* with the Father, Jesus Christ the righteous" (1 John 2:1, emphasis added; important JST addition in caps).

This great blessing of additional intercession clearly depends on the adequacy of our personal faith and repentance, if we are also to receive God's greatest gift, eternal life (D&C 6:13; 14:7).

The entirety of Jesus' unique role as advocate cannot be understood if approached only legalistically and adversarily, such as when one mortal lawyer jousts with another lawyer before an impassive judge. In the sense here intended, an advocate seeks to plead, to persuade, to intercede, and to mediate in order to aid another's cause. This is surely part of what Jesus does for us. But He is, once again, both the advocate and the judge! No mortal lawyer has such a dual role.

When commencing the agonies of the Atonement, Jesus declared of His atoning purpose, "For this cause came I into the world" (John 18:37).

In calling upon the mercy available in Father's plan, Jesus thereby truly "advocateth the cause of the children of men" (Moroni 7:28). It is significant that He so pleads for us out of His full, personal knowledge and understanding of each of us, including our individual experiences and short-falls set amid the shared general human condition. "Behold, and hearken, . . . saith the Lord your God, even Jesus Christ, your advocate, who knoweth the weakness of man and how to succor them who are tempted" (D&C 62:1).

He can succor us in any form of the human condition because, as He reminded Joseph in the Liberty jail: "The Son of Man hath descended below them all. Art thou greater than he?" (D&C 122:8.) No person, therefore, who comes before Him can exclaim, "You don't understand what I have been through!"

How like the tender words cited earlier (D&C 45:3-5) are the following and amplifying words recorded in Alma, attesting to Jesus' personal knowledge of our individual and personal sufferings and sicknesses:

> And he shall go forth, suffering pains and afflictions and temptations of every kind; and this that the word might be fulfilled which saith he will take upon him the pains and the sicknesses of his people.
>
> And he will take upon him death, that he may loose the bands of death which bind his people; and he will take upon him their infirmities, that his bowels may be filled with mercy, according to the flesh, that he may know according to the flesh how to succor his people according to their infirmities. (Alma 7:11-12. See also Matthew 8:17.)

Hence Jesus not only bore our sins personally in order to atone for them, but He also bore our pains, infirmities, and afflictions. Thereby ensured is the precious fact that Jesus' mercy would be full, because He knows how to succor us in a unique, merciful, and personal way—amid all of that through which we mortals individually pass. Having so purchased us once, His glad and great investment in us continues (see Acts 20:28).

For example, many in various illnesses have measured their recovery in such small degrees and over so many days—like the hand-over-hand climb out of a steep gravel pit. But Jesus' empathy is not merely a matter of detached intellectual familiarity. He helps us, hand over hand, because He understands personally that through which we pass. No wonder we should acknowledge His hand.

Therefore, beyond ensuring general immortality if, as to our sins, we are adequately and truly repentant, He likewise specifically succors and pleads for us as only He can. He does this out of His perfect love, a love which is fully informed by His perfect, personal familiarity with our individual situations. No wonder He is the wondrous Keeper of the entering gate to eternal life, and in His loving empathy He "employeth no servant there" (see 2 Nephi 9:41).

However, for our own good, and since terms are "affixed," He does not exempt us entirely from experiencing justice (see 2 Nephi 2:10). Instead, given the role of judgment, which the Father has delegated to Him, Christ balances the twin considerations of mercy and justice in each of our cases (see John 5:22). Besides, we must come to understand personally the twin and eternal principles of justice and mercy if we are to help Him with His work in eternity, which is "one eternal round" (see 1 Nephi 10:19).

His empathy for us is expansive because He understands with a fulness of knowledge that we did not bring about our own fallen condition; thus He unconditionally redeems us from physical death and provides the opportunity for our eventual redemption. Though we do not understand the end from the beginning, He does; therefore our shortcomings are too often caused by our short-sightedness and "blindness of minds."

Divine justice assures that there are no loopholes through which the not-fully-worthy would slip undeservedly into the celestial kingdom, where they would not be fully happy anyway. The plan of happiness is carefully gauged, blessing all, but especially those who have "faith unto repentance."

For the repentant righteous, a fulness of divine mercy as to the celestial kingdom finally prevails:

> And thus he shall bring salvation *to all those who shall believe on his name*; this being the intent of this last sacrifice, to bring about the bowels of *mercy, which overpowereth justice*, and bringeth about means unto men that they may have *faith unto repentance* (Alma 34:15; emphasis added).

Without the overriding and glorious assurance in Father's plan, it would be difficult, indeed, for us to have the personal capacity to develop "faith unto repentance" (Alma 34:16). Unlike fatalism ("Why bother to repent?"), such faith moves us to the needed personal contrition. Therefore, so far as drawing upon Jesus' atonement is concerned, those most valiant in their testimonies of Jesus will clearly be those who benefit the most by having the most "faith unto repentance," sufficient in order to become more like Him. (See Alma 34:15-17; Helaman 15:7; D&C 19:31; 53:3.)

Jesus knows and takes into account, personally and perfectly, the highly individualized situations of our "tether and pang," including the innermost desires and intents of our hearts, and including the comparative constraints within which we function. In a unique way, therefore, Jesus' ongoing and authentic pleadings are received by a loving Father with His own perfect and especially "tender mercies" (see 1 Nephi 1:20; D&C 45:3-5).

Even so, as already noted, the bestowal of full divine mercy necessary for the celestial kingdom is conditional: "But behold, I, Nephi, will show unto you that the tender mercies of the Lord are over all those whom he hath chosen, *because of their faith,* to make them mighty even unto the power of deliverance" (1 Nephi 1:20; emphasis added).

One of the great examples of His intercessory role on behalf of all those who believe on the words of the Apostles is that they can have the same reward as the original and witnessing Twelve received (see John 17; see also D&C 93).

Thus, as can be seen, Jesus' pleading in our behalf constitutes anything but a ritualistic brush-by. In order for Christ to be able to plead fully and justifiably, we are to be fully repentant. In Heavenly Father's plan, real repentance thus satisfies the divine requirement of justice and likewise entitles us to His divine mercy. Hence the Son's advocacy, performed with perfect empathy, both satisfies justice and evokes perfect mercy. Jesus' full comprehension thus brought to pass a fully comprehensive atonement, indeed, an "infinite atonement" (2 Nephi 25:16; 9:7; Alma 34:12).

Hence we see how Jesus is our advocate in the most unique way. After all, if all this were analogous to mere mortal advocacy, how many advocates know their clients perfectly? For example, how many mortal advocates have actually suffered deeply, physically and mentally, for their clients? Besides all this, we are not mere clients. We are Christ's spirit brothers and sisters!

No wonder the Savior's advocacy is so uniquely persuasive, powerful, and pleading. No wonder both justice and mercy will be so uniquely balanced by the Father and the Son.

Of Their divine roles, President Harold B. Lee wisely said:

The apostle Paul in his writings to the Corinthians taught that "there be gods many, and lords many," and then he added, "But to us there is but one God, the Father, *of whom* are all things, and we in him; and one Lord Jesus Christ, *by whom* are all things, and we by him." (1 Cor. 8:5-6. Italics added.)

I would have you note particularly the use of the preposition "of," in reference to the Father, and the preposition "by," in reference to our Lord, Jesus Christ. In this statement is clearly defined the role of each, the Lord to do the bidding of the Father, in the execution of the whole plan of salvation for all mankind. (See Abr. 4.) ("Time to Prepare to Meet God," *Improvement Era,* December 1970, p. 29.)

Therefore, as has been said, "In [Christ] all things hold together" (RSV, Colossians 1:17).

Christ's accomplishment of the Atonement was a glorious, one-time, supernal event! Of His atonement, He declared in *past tense*, "I partook and finished my preparations unto the children of men" (D&C 19:19). In confirmation there was His conclusive cry on the cross: "It is finished" (John 19:30).

However, unlike the "finished" act of the Atonement achieved in that axis of atoning agony—Gethsemane and on Calvary—across an additional time frame Jesus' continuing advocacy for us mortals is spread. It continues in a special, ongoing process as we, individually, access and apply His atoning blood. (See Mosiah 4:1-4.) Having paid the price for us, the Grand Atoner is also the apparent judge as to our entitlement to access further His atonement, as we repent and become "the children of Christ" (Mosiah 5:7).

Jesus did not retire to some corner of the universe for a well-earned vacation after performing the great Atonement, but He has remained constantly vigilant and vigorous, personally mindful of all of us.

Before the world was, Jesus clearly knew the Father's plan of redemption would be necessary. Jesus volunteered to be the Redeemer, while pledging to give all the glory to the Father (Moses 4:2). The real question, back then, was not "Is a Savior needed?" Rather, it was "Who will be the Savior?" Who would submissively carry out the Father's plan in full accordance with the Father's will? Jesus, being sinless and being the Firstborn of the Eternal Father in the spirit world, was utterly and uniquely qualified to perform the Atonement. No one else was qualified in full conformance with the Father's will; "there was no other good enough" ("There Is a Green Hill Far Away," *Hymns*, no. 194).

Christ's role of advocacy was evident long before the atoning agonies of Gethsemane and Calvary in the meridian of time. Consider this illustrative revelation, indicating His premortal pleading as the Messiah in behalf of the wicked of Noah's time:

> And That which I have chosen *hath pled* before my face. Wherefore, he suffereth for their sins; inasmuch as they will repent in the day that my Chosen shall return unto me, and until that day they shall be in torment (Moses 7:39; emphasis added).

The people of Noah's time were not alone in receiving Jesus' particularized advocacy, being joined by those much later Saints of 1831.

> Listen to him who is the advocate with the Father, who *is pleading* your cause before him—
>
> Saying: Father, behold the sufferings and death of him who did no sin, in whom thou wast well pleased; behold the blood of thy Son which was shed, the blood of him whom thou gavest that thyself might be glorified;
>
> Wherefore, Father, spare these my brethren that believe on my name, that they may come unto me and have everlasting life (D&C 45:3-5; emphasis added).

Others can and do plead, too, of course, but not in the unique way of our Perfect Redeemer.

On how many other occasions before and after the great Atonement has Jesus pleaded? We do not know, but His was surely an "infinite atonement"!

Jesus, who knows our weaknesses, is thus our perfectly empathetic Advocate with the Father, judging who among us is qualified to receive the necessary divine mercy. It is significant that mercy can bring to us a very much needed and precious personal blessing and assurance: our knowing of a certainty that we have been forgiven! Thereby we are enabled to continue our spiritual progress, instead of allowing our souls to "droop" forever in sin, including by experiencing, as some do, the immobilizing and disabling "sorrowing of the damned" (Mormon 2:13).

It is not only we spiritual lessers who need to know we have been forgiven, but also such spiritual luminaries as Peter, Paul, and Alma the Younger, all of whom needed to know they were forgiven by Jesus of their frailties in order to better carry out their significant and special ministries. How full of praise we should be for this grand gift of divine forgiveness!

While the scriptures relevant to Jesus' advocacy are abundant, verb tenses vary, as already noted, suggesting something significant. For further examples consider the *post-atonement* scriptures, such as Hebrews 7:25, which declares that Jesus "*ever liveth* to make intercession," suggesting a continuousness. Hebrews 9:24 speaks of how He *is to appear* to make intercession for us, perhaps at the day of judgment. The Apostle John wrote that *if we sin, we have an advocate* with the Father, likewise suggesting an ongoingness to Jesus' advocacy and to our accessing and applying His atonement (1 John 2:1). Moroni 7:28 notes Christ's atonement and declares that He "*advocateth* the cause of the children of men." Doctrine and Covenants 45:3-5, as noted earlier, indicates that He "*is pleading*" in our behalf, again the indication of an ongoingness.

Hence His pleading apparently continues for all specific and worthy individuals until the final judgment. Hear Elder Bruce R. McConkie as to Christ's "interceding petitions."

> Jesus pleads the cause of the Twelve—and all the saints—in the courts above. He is their Mediator, Advocate, and Intercessor. He makes intercession for them, because they have forsaken the world and come unto him; he advocates their cause, for their cause is his cause and they have received his gospel; he performs a divine service of mediation, reconciling fallen man to his Maker, because the fallen ones choose now to associate with those who are not of this world. Jesus prays, thus, not for the world, but for those who have kept his commandments; who have reconciled themselves to God through faith and repentance; who are preparing themselves for an abode with him and his Father. *And his interceding petitions are always available for all men, if they will but believe his word and obey his law.* (*The Mortal Messiah,* 4 vols. [Salt Lake City: Deseret Book Co., 1979–81], 4:111; emphasis added.)

Not only are we to renounce sin and to cease sinning, but also we are to become more like Him, further entitling us to His advocacy. To His disciples Jesus gave a "new commandment"—to love one another *as He had loved them* (John 13:34). This was and is a high standard, more than

loving others as oneself. Is not having such serious discipleship, which helps us to come unto Christ, the predicate for
His mediation?

Hence Jesus' advocacy appears to be a continuing
process, as we struggle individually to overcome our weakness and thereby to "apply the atoning blood of Christ" by
becoming more like Him (Mosiah 4:2).

Thus while the act of the great and glorious Atonement
itself is over, including Jesus' immense Gethsemane-
Calvary suffering, our individual suffering will be ongoing
unless we regularly access the awaiting benefits of the great
Atonement (Mosiah 4:2; see also Mosiah 3:11, 15, 16;
Alma 21:9; Helaman 5:9). This further indication of ongoingness is seen in Jesus' truly promising us that if we repent
we need not suffer as He suffered (D&C 19:17). It is Jesus,
therefore, who in an ongoing way advocates our cause with
the Father. Jesus emancipates us not only from everlasting
death but from needless, present suffering from sin, too.

Christ purchased us with His blood, and thereby we
have become His. Thus He became our lawgiver and the
terms setter, the terms being non-negotiable. What mercy
we receive, proximately and ultimately, will be based on our
degree of compliance with His commandments. Surely,
therefore, Jesus—advocate and judge—is not disinterested
in applying justice, for if we were not thereby improved
adequately, we could not truly feel we belonged to the
Father and to Him as the children of Christ, obedient to
His will. (See Mosiah 5:2-7.)

Jesus' premortal and ongoing willingness to be our
advocate will be joined by His final attestation at the final
judgment, verifying in behalf of all the worthy.

And these things doth the Spirit manifest unto me; therefore I write unto you all. And for this cause I write unto you, that ye may know that ye must all stand before *the judgment-seat of Christ*, yea, every soul who belongs to the whole human family of Adam; and ye must stand to be judged of your works, whether they be good or evil. (Mormon 3:20; emphasis added.)

Not only was Jesus' atonement highly personal, because of our burdens that He bore in that grand moment in the meridian of time, but His further advocacy is likewise highly personal. We do not know the details of that ongoing process, but it is precious and personal, too. Recall, again, that the Father has "committed all judgment" to the Son to effect this unparalleled emancipation and the great gift of eternal life! (John 5:22.)

Of course, the Father knew beforehand of all human wickedness. He knew beforehand of mankind's need of a Savior. He knows the past, present, and future, since all their dimensions are continually before Him, said the Prophet Joseph Smith, constituting "one eternal 'now'" (*Teachings of the Prophet Joseph Smith*, sel. Joseph Fielding Smith [Salt Lake City: Deseret Book Co., 1938], p. 220; see also 1 Nephi 10:19; D&C 3:2; 35:1). Therefore, mortal sins previously committed and those yet to be committed were atoned for *retroactively* and *prospectively* in Gethsemane and on Calvary. For us of the last dispensation, it was "paid in advance," as it were. However, the individual sinner is still left with his own need to claim that divine payment by meeting the conditions set by Christ, thus working through those sins, as prescribed, by currently applying the atoning blood of Jesus.

Drenched with meaning, that phrase "committed all judgment" implies that Jesus, Himself, is doing His Father's will in the balancing of both justice and mercy. After having done so, He can then advocate and certify to the Father at the final judgment that the process required of Him is complete—especially advocating for those whose personal wills have, by then, been sufficiently "swallowed up" in the will of the Father (Mosiah 15:7).

So it is that "after all we can do," we still depend on the glorious, glad fact that, finally, "mercy . . . overpowereth justice" (Alma 34:15). No wonder we should "praise Him for His mercy" and do so unceasingly! Besides, none of us is so constantly error-free that we do not constantly need to ask for divine mercy and forgiveness.

Praise him for his mer - cy; Praise him for his love.

For un-num-bered bless - ings Praise the Lord a - bove.

Let our hap - py voic - es Still the notes pro - long.

One a - lone is wor - thy Of our sweet-est song.

CHAPTER FOUR

"Praise Him for His Mercy"

When we speak of praising God, the Father, and His Son, Jesus Christ, such praise should constitute much more than ritualistic incantations or merely saying nice things about God. The more specific and frequent our praise, the better. Instead, too, such praise should proceed from the whole soul, because of a dawning realization of all that God has done, is doing, and will yet do for all His children as well as for us personally (see Moroni 10:3).

There are good reasons, therefore, why the first commandment is first and the second commandment is second. Of course we are to *love* our neighbors, but we *do not worship* them, nor do we glorify them. Yes, the second commandment is "like unto the first," but it is not the first! We worship and glorify the Perfect Objects of the first commandment, but, though we are to love Them, we do not in turn worship the imperfect objects of the second commandment! There is to be reverent recognition of the towering supremacy of God, the divine and perfect

Object of the love spoken of in the first commandment.

Moreover, if we love God with all of our heart, might, *mind*, and strength, this requires one's intellectual surrender to God, too. Alas, while still too few, there are still comparatively more knees bent in reverence to God than there are minds. Hence there are more people who partially keep the second commandment than truly keep the first. It is the first commandment that sets the high tone and the standards, enabling the second to be "like unto" it. Otherwise, every man would walk in his own way and do his own thing, which might include some useful—but sidebar—service to his fellow mortals (D&C 1:16).

One's realization about Jesus' role may commence with only an *acknowledgment* of Him and ripen into real *appreciation*, then into deep *admiration,* and then proceed into genuine *adoration* and, finally, into reverent *emulation.* Our ultimate praise, therefore, is to pattern our lives after His.

The best way to reach out for Christ is by taking His hand firmly and constantly! He has said encouragingly to us, "I will lead you along," because "ye cannot bear all things now" (D&C 78:18).

If meek, we will see more keenly and completely the full range of God's goodness to us. We will feel the depth of His love for us and will experience the manifestations of His loving-kindness in our behalf. No wonder we will praise Jesus "forever and ever." (D&C 133:52.) Nephi, as already noted, clearly knew of God's goodness, including from his early life.

I, Nephi, having been born of goodly parents, therefore I was taught somewhat in all the learning of my father; and having seen many afflictions in the course of my days, nevertheless, having been highly favored of the Lord in all my days; yea, having had a great knowledge of the goodness and the mysteries of God, therefore I make a record of my proceedings in my days (1 Nephi 1:1).

For myself, therefore, I searchingly ask, "Have I praised Him often enough?" Especially for any small success I have achieved? And, even when I have praised Him, "have I specifically and genuinely given the honor and the glory to Him?" What He wants from us is not superficial incantations but heartfelt awareness of His causality as it really is.

There are so many examples of His "tender care," including His guiding hand even in micro matters. Thus it is important for us to acknowledge His hand not only in the governance of the galaxies but also in His "overseeing" details of our lives while still preserving our agency.

Therefore, to praise Him is to have faith in His timing as well as in His purposes. This includes faith in this timing and purposes even when our tactical situations are stress-filled, even if not fully like Lehi's in the wilderness, or like Moses' on the edge of the tempestuous Red Sea, or like the anxious young man with Elisha on a mount surrounded by the enemy's horses and chariots (see 2 Kings 6).

Thus when we experience tactical chastening at His hands, this chastening is part of His hastening. He is accelerating the finishing and polishing of our souls. When the Lord says of the mortal experience that He will prove us "herewith," He means "in this manner." Of his experience the Prophet Joseph Smith said of the process:

I am like a huge, rough stone rolling down from a high mountain; and the only polishing I get is when some corner gets rubbed off by coming in contact with something else, striking with accelerated force . . . —all hell knocking off a corner here and a corner there. Thus I will become a smooth and polished shaft in the quiver of the Almighty. (*Teachings of the Prophet Joseph Smith*, sel. Joseph Fielding Smith [Salt Lake City: Deseret Book Co., 1938], p. 304.)

No wonder so many scriptures emphasize the importance of our coming to know God and what He is like, including why He tutors us. Yet some believe in Him, but only as an unknowable abstraction. Actually, however, considerations of life eternal are involved in really striving to know Him, since to know God is "life eternal," just as Jesus declared in His great high priestly prayer (John 17:3). In fact, in order to comprehend ourselves it is essential to comprehend God's character, said the Prophet Joseph (see *Teachings of the Prophet Joseph Smith*, p. 343).

In facilitating such further knowing of Him, it helps greatly to do as King Lamoni's father did; he was willing to "give away all [his] sins to know" Him (Alma 22:18). Clearing away the personal underbrush of unworthiness is essential, for it makes progress possible in moving from acknowledgment to appreciation on to admiration and from admiration to adoration and on to emulation.

Therefore, our knowing what God is like is as vital as our knowing that He lives! No wonder God has so carefully revealed Himself and His character in various theophanies, revelations, and scriptures. Not only is it our task to search and ponder all of these instructive insights, but it is also to apply these revelations developmentally and personally. In this process we are to "liken these scriptures," with their illustrative attributes and qualities, "unto ourselves" (see 1 Nephi 19:23).

Doing this is so much more than merely reciting a litany of God's perfected attributes and qualities. Another serious shortfall, however, would be to view these divine attributes as forever unattainable by us in any significant degree, as if the qualities cited in the Sermon on the Mount represented a totally unscalable mountain, so why try? (See Matthew 5:48; 3 Nephi 12:48.)

It was George MacDonald who pointed out a parallel challenge—the irony that if we have a wrong concept of God, we can end up mistakenly serving our own self-centeredness rather than serving Him. Some, MacDonald wrote, are simply not able to serve a God higher than they are capable of imagining. Thinking too little of one's own identity and possibilities can turn one aside from the trek up the mountain. Either way we lose! Tents are pitched far too soon.

In fact, actually coming to know of God's attributes, such as goodness and mercy, draws us to Him and can actually lead us unto repentance (see Romans 2:4). The Lord so confirmed, saying, "Yea, I have loved thee with an everlasting love; therefore with lovingkindness have I drawn thee" (Jeremiah 31:3).

As we come to know God, the Father, and Jesus Christ, His Only Begotten Son, we desire to become evermore like Them, attribute by attribute. We are clearly directed by Him to become more of that manner of individual who is, indeed, "even as [He is]" (3 Nephi 27:27; see also Matthew 5:48; 3 Nephi 12:48; 2 Peter 3:11).

No wonder, to repeat, the Prophet Joseph Smith taught, "If men do not comprehend the character of God, they do not comprehend themselves" (*Teachings of the Prophet Joseph Smith*, p. 343). How can children really and fully know themselves anyway without knowing their Father? In their search for faith, a great many mortals truly stumble precisely because of an incorrect understanding about God (see 1 Nephi 14:1).

No wonder a single but powerful gospel concept can matter so much. In the *Lectures on Faith* we are told that in order to have faith we must first know that He exists but second know His attributes of character (*Lectures on Faith* 3:4).

The Restoration, among other things, removes stumbling blocks and provides much additional truth concerning both the character of the Father and the nature of His plan for His children (see 1 Nephi 14:1). Elder George Q. Cannon observed: "There is in the plan of salvation, which God our heavenly Father has revealed, perfect love, mercy and justice, and every other attribute which pertains to the character of Deity are perfectly illustrated in the plan of salvation which he has revealed for man's guidance" (in *Journal of Discourses* 14:312; see also Moses 7:30). Nevertheless, Elder Cannon lamented, "The difficulty today is, that the people do not believe that God is a being of this character" (in *Journal of Discourses* 15:371).

Hence, by way of selecting but a single, illustrative focal point, let us particularly examine one divine attribute: mercy. This quality is not trendy, yet it is vital. Of course it is to be balanced with justice; but having already so indicated, let us speak illustratively of mercy.

To begin with, we have only to reflect upon what happens when there is a general absence of mercy. Whenever selfishness flexes, for example, it soon squeezes out mercy and generosity. Likewise, when pride pulsates, it quickly and rudely pushes both mercy and meekness out of the way. In contrast, in a world more starved for love than food, how precious is the gracious individual who overlooks our weaknesses and mercifully clothes us instead in the much-needed "garment of praise" (Isaiah 61:3). While we cannot, by ourselves, change weaknesses in others, we can help to lift them up in order that they might see more clearly what is commendable about them, thus giving them some hope and reason to rejoice. So many hands "hang down" (see D&C 81:5).

Because iniquity is increasing in the world, however, not only will the love of many wax cold, but so will mercy and compassion decline (see Matthew 24:12; D&C 45:27). Yet mercy is such a precious, enabling, and essential virtue, hence "whosoever repenteth shall find mercy, and he that findeth mercy and endureth to the end the same shall be saved" (Alma 32:13; see also Luke 6:36; Matthew 5:7). We surely need mercy in order to be able to endure. The virtues are all linked together, interwoven with a tensile strength, which keeps all things "fitly framed together" (Ephesians 2:21; 4:16).

Of course, on this mortal stage we do see some special and inspiring moments of mercy. Nevertheless, as the love of many waxes cold, vengeance and "getting even" will increasingly be the actuating focus as too many mortals end up being "without mercy" (Moroni 9:18).

We would be surprised if we knew how persistently the unmerciful natural man, even if once deposed, still runs alongside us, hoping to remount by throwing his saddle on us once again. Though we may have once "put off" the natural man, if we allow ourselves to be so re-saddled, mercy quickly dismounts and departs. (See Mosiah 3:19.)

How much human history would be different if the quality of mercy were more valued? How many "unconditional surrenders" followed by Versaille-like vengeance have merely ended up igniting more wars? And how many solutions to society's complex problems go unrealized, because the search for vindication takes preeminence over extending mercy? How much political campaigning seizes upon an opponent's error, "Gotcha!", rather than extending a merciful slowness to judge?

It is deeply relevant that, when Enoch actually saw the God of Heaven weep over unnecessary human suffering, he proclaimed specifically over two of God's attributes, saying, "Thou art merciful and kind forever" (see Moses 7:30).

It surely is not surprising that those who have been mentored through their own "fiery furnaces" are the warmest in their praise of God for His "tender mercies."

> But thou, O Lord, art a God full of *compassion*, and *gracious*, *longsuffering*, and plenteous in *mercy* and *truth* (Psalm 86:15; emphasis added).

> O give thanks unto the Lord; for he is *good*; for his *mercy* endureth for ever" (Psalm 136:1; emphasis added).

> . . . The Lord God, merciful and *gracious*, *longsuffering*,

and abundant in *goodness* and *truth* (Exodus 34:6; emphasis added).

> The Lord is not slack, . . . but is *longsuffering* to us-ward, not willing that any should perish, but that all should come to repentance (2 Peter 3:9; emphasis added).

Thus, as one ripples through the pages of scriptures, his soul ripples with appreciation, for we really can know that God *is*, but also what He *is like!*

In the final judgment, *all* mortals will finally and freely acknowledge that God is God, including those who have lived "without God in the world" (Alma 41:11). The grateful chorus, as every knee bows and every tongue confesses that Jesus is the Christ, will cite the perfection of God's justice and mercy (Alma 12:15; Mosiah 16:1; 27:31). Furthermore, after all the considerations of justice have been fully cared for, noted once again there is this stunning assurance: "Mercy . . . overpowereth justice"! (Alma 34:15.)

Meanwhile, for us, awareness of God's ultimate mercy is needed, operationally, such as in order to overcome any resentment we may have of mortal injustices that impact upon us—perceived or real. The quality of mercy is also needed in us in order to dissolve any reservations we may have over the welcoming attention, rightly given, to returning prodigals and to sinners restored. Our forgetting is our sunshine ray of mercy that hastens the new growth of hope in others.

Who dares to infer, therefore, that mercy is merely a passive and limp virtue?

Miserable at first, Alma actually desired his extinction.

But in a happy moment he remembered the words of his father about a prospective and atoning Jesus. This caused Alma's later and great soul cry: "Now, as my mind caught hold upon this thought, I cried within my heart: O Jesus, thou Son of God, have mercy on me." (Alma 36:15-18.) Let us not be surprised, therefore, when we all plead for mercy.

Being merciful with each other is especially vital whenever we or others are on the pathway of repentance. We do not, for instance, criticize patients in intensive care for looking pale, patched, and preoccupied. Why then those recovering from needed surgery on their souls? No need for us to stare; those ugly, distracting stitches will finally come out.

In life's hospital, too, it is so important to remember that "the chart is not the patient." Thus the act of extending mercy should not be abstract, proforma, and paper-centered, nor should mercy wait upon our full understanding of another's challenges! Moreover, whether or not it is appreciated or reciprocated, mercy is never wasted! Even at the apogee of His agony, Jesus, nevertheless, mercifully consoled one thief who hung beside Him, saying, "Today shalt thou be with me in paradise" (Luke 23:43).

In God's infinite mercy and generosity, "the glory of the telestial" will surpass "all understanding" (D&C 76:89). Furthermore, our family circles, when finally assembled in the celestial world to come, may yet be larger than some currently distressed and disappointed parents may now imagine; late arrivals, after having paid a severe price, may constitute more than just a few. "Oh, the greatness of the mercy of our God!" (2 Nephi 9:19.) If, however, Jesus' mercy were merely episodic like ours, His arm would not be constantly and reassuringly "lengthened out all the day long" (2 Nephi 28:32).

Therefore, in view of how vital mercy is, a person should take exceeding care that his mortal activities do not take him in an opposite developmental direction. Desensitizing circumstances, for example, will not help us in fostering the attribute of mercy. Neither will striving for status and preeminence, nor cutthroat competition, nor macho brusqueness! Such situations and expressions are to be shunned, for these will make us strangers to the Master and His mercy (Mosiah 5:13).

So it is that "in process of time," by interactive "mercy and truth [that] iniquity is purged" (Proverbs 16:6). In companying with truth, mercy is not uncaring indulgence. No wonder we read, "What doth the Lord require of thee, but to do justly, and to love mercy, and to walk humbly with thy God?" (Micah 6:8.)

Mercy similarly requires the companionship of patience. A repentant Nineveh was mercifully not destroyed, which provided a great lesson not only in the tutoring of Jonah but for us, too. Mercy rejoices in every step taken toward righteousness. Mercy is not easily offended and will gladly give place for such first, faltering steps.

Any exemplifying mercy can prove contagious. Following his "testimony of Jesus Christ," as Stephen was being slain, he behaved with mercy reminiscent of his Lord, Jesus ("Father, forgive them; for they know not what they do"), saying, "Lord, lay not this sin to their charge" (Acts 7:60).

Relevant, personal experience induces greater mercy. Helen Keller said in her quiet but wonderful way that chastening "tear[s] away the blindfold of indifference from our eyes, and we behold the burdens others are carrying" (*Light in My Darkness* [West Chester, Pa.: Chrysalis Books, 1927/1994], p. 135). Helen Keller speaks, too, of how the soil of adversity is required in order for the "violets of patience and sweetness" to grow (*Light in My Darkness*, p. 135.) Hence the Lord will see to it that we have certain tutoring experiences.

The mercy-filled and moving statement by Jesus: "O Jerusalem, Jerusalem," reflected centuries of unresponsiveness toward Jehovah/Jesus on the part of ancient Israel (Matthew 23:37). Whoever constituted His immediate audience on that day of that lamentation, they were, in a sense, merely stand-ins for earlier and larger throngs. But mercy was extended even when it was unappreciated—a lesson for us on our smaller scale.

However, if mercy is merely regarded as something we would like to work on starting next month, or if it seems too grand or too intimidating even to try, how about your and my considering extending at least some small modicums of mercy as a start? For instance, let's offer the garment of deserved praise to one with whom we have recently differed (Isaiah 61:3). Or, let's quickly accept even that which may seem to be a grudging, ritualistic apology with genuine and expressive mercy. Or, likewise, let's quickly and obviously forget an offense, so that we actually and specifically "give place" for the doer of the misdeed by doing our part to facilitate his general reclassification.

Seventy times seven is not only the standard rule for

forgiveness; it also applies to the repeated need for extensions of mercy! (See Matthew 18:22.) Mercy requires of us that we sometimes be willing to take the initiative by patting a porcupine. If we acquire any quill marks, these are merely evidence of a scarred but helping hand of fellowship.

Mercy, even so, is not naiveté. Nor is it uncaring indulgence. Nor is mercy to be mistaken for today's standardless and indulgent tolerance. Divine mercy has its fixed divine standards intact. When Jesus said, "Father, forgive them; for they know not what they do," He was mercifully and forgivingly acknowledging what was, nevertheless, an ignorantly induced but terrible wrong! (Luke 23:34.)

In any case, whenever we can, using the lubricant of mercy, let us meekly remove ourselves as any kind of a stumbling block in the path of progress of others. Besides, we are not yet error free ourselves. Hence we all need to plead for mercy as we sincerely plead, "Save us, Lord, from error." Our sincere pleas will be heard by Those who are merciful and perfect, a fact most needed and reassuring!

CHAPTER FIVE

■

"Save Us, Lord, from Error"

"Jesus, our Redeemer, now our praises hear" should include our worshipful gratitude for His purity, which purity, of necessity, underwrote His glorious and stunning atonement. Since we are to become a pure people, the need for our own ever-greater personal purity thus comes boldly to the fore, as we "liken all scriptures unto us" (1 Nephi 19:23).

On the Western Hemisphere, centuries ago, Jesus asked, "Therefore, what manner of men ought ye to be? Verily I say unto you, even as I am." (3 Nephi 27:27.)

Jesus sacrificed His Perfect Self so that we could be redeemed. This was His to do, because, as we sing, "There was no other good enough to pay the price of sin" ("There Is a Green Hill Far Away," *Hymns*, no. 194).

Since Christ gave Himself in all His perfection for the expiation of our imperfections, we can at least "give away all [our] sins" (Alma 22:18). It is this process, the discarding of our errors that is so much a part of the losing of our old selves, by means of which we actually find ourselves!

What a tight and hard knot our sins and weaknesses can become, however. Vices as well as virtues are interactive. It was George MacDonald who observed, "The self is given to us that we may sacrifice it . . . that we, like Christ, may have somewhat to offer" (*George MacDonald: An Anthology*, ed. C. S. Lewis [New York: Macmillan], 1947, p. 69). Letting our wills be swallowed up in God's pure will is the essence of this yielding (Mosiah 15:7).

In order to become "even as Jesus is," we should strive to develop what Paul called "the mind of Christ," which is perfectly pure (1 Corinthians 2:16). Though Jesus suffered "temptations of every kind," He "gave no heed unto them" (D&C 20:22; Mosiah 3:7; Alma 7:11-12). Therefore, to become "even as [He is]" requires that "virtue garnish [our] thoughts unceasingly" (D&C 121:45). The demanding word, *unceasingly*, is clearly related to Jesus' regularly and dismissively giving temptation "no heed." These two conditions constitute the great "How to's" so essential to cleanliness of mind and purity of soul. They signify "a mighty change of heart" (see Alma 5:12). They can bring us to a point where we lose the desire for sin and have no more disposition to do evil (Mosiah 5:2).

Grossness in conduct is preceded by grossness of mind. Ironic though it is, ultimately those so warped by pleasing the carnal mind and by wrongfully celebrating their capacity to feel soon lose their capacity to feel, finally becoming "past feeling" (1 Nephi 17:45; Moroni 9:20).

Our Exemplar shows the way, for without Jesus' infinite purity there could have been no "infinite atonement" (2 Nephi 9:7). In fact, the gift of our resurrection depended upon His purity.

In our time, as in Lot's of old, we are vexed by many things, including profane and filthy conversation (2 Peter 2:7). We hear intrusive things we wish we would not hear and which we must dismiss and deflect in order to give "no heed." Sometimes giving rebuke or actually leaving such company are clearly called for.

Avoidance of those things that distance us from Jesus and that disqualify us from having His Spirit include the improper use of videos, music, Internet, and printed filth— all these are "off limits" for us. Pornography can not only lead to child and spouse abuse, but it steadily sucks out one's spiritual bone marrow. The adversary gets some individuals to rationalize concerning their privacy, agency, and individuality by lessening their sense of accountability for their wrongful indulging. Then there is the multiplier as to consequences, for sin hurts at least one soul and almost always more. Especially when the toll from the sins of omission is tallied. If only such withheld time and talent had not been "omitted" but otherwise used! (See Matthew 23:23.)

My second mission president, Floyed G. Eyre, advised us that while a person may not always be able to keep an impure thought from entering his mind, he needn't offer it a chair and invite it to sit down. This is an initial dimension of giving "no heed," which can be so useful and practical. If there is no first step toward the "gulf of misery," there will never be a second or third.

A searching interrogatory by Benjamin occurs in his superb sermon, and it is eloquently expressed: "For how knoweth a man the master whom he has not served, and who is a stranger unto him, and is far from the thoughts and intents of his heart?" (Mosiah 5:13.)

Discipleship really does require extensive thinking about, praying to, and serving the Lord. Otherwise, distance develops; and distance deprives us. There can be no deep discipleship if we do not have heartfelt intentions concerning Him; otherwise, the estrangement will engulf us. Instead, it should be, "Jesus, the very thought of thee with sweetness fills my breast" ("Jesus, the Very Thought of Thee," *Hymns*, no. 141).

Thus, if one "mind[s] the things of the flesh," he simply cannot "have the mind of Christ" (Romans 8:5; 1 Corinthians 2:16). Errant thought patterns cause us to stray "far from" Jesus; irrelevant thought patterns do too, though less far.

In multiple scriptures, a dual assignment is given to the Church members. We are to both "build up" the Church and kingdom, and also to "establish the [Lord's] righteousness" (JST, Matthew 6:38). Society may be becoming more decadent, but nevertheless we can further "establish" the Lord's patterns and standards of righteousness, including purity in our own individual lives. We can help do likewise in our families, and even help in our neighborhoods and wards. Without adequate individual moral cleanliness, however, there can be no personal righteousness, no little family Zions, and none of the much-needed clusters of the "pure in heart."

One major reason why "the love of many shall wax cold" in our time is uncleanliness (Matthew 24:12). Charity and purity go together more than we realize. In Sodom and Gomorrah the poor and the needy were neglected. (Ezekiel 16:49.) Why? Because those self-centered people were so preoccupied with pleasing themselves, including with inordinate filth. If we mind the things of the flesh too much, then our own flesh and blood will mean much less to us. Furthermore, the needs of neighbors will not easily occur to carnally-filled minds.

One of the first messages given to the first prophet in this last dispensation included the warning about how some would "teach for doctrines the commandments of men" arising out of the "persuasions of men" (D&C 46:7; 3:7; Matthew 15:9; Mark 7:7; Joseph Smith—History 1:19). Even when the commandments of men are not necessarily evil, they are lesser laws. Moreover, the *in lieu* commandments of men usually spawn many secular regulations, thereby multiplying and reflecting the lower ways of a lower world. (D&C 46:7; Colossians 2:22.)

One important way, therefore, in which the Church is to be "independent" involves distancing ourselves from the philosophies and persuasions of men, and from the encompassing and enveloping ways of secular societies (D&C 78:14). Secularism recruits so easily, because so many mortals "will not endure sound doctrine," but come to prefer the easier and more fashionable "commandments of men" (2 Timothy 4:3; Matthew 15:9). But, of course, the fashions of the world will pass away. It will be interesting to see, for instance, how long America can sustain an inspired and constraining Constitution, if more of the people it governs become persistently permissive. Will what is now the "lesser part" reach a critical, negative mass? (See Mosiah 29.)

Coming to have "the mind of Christ" clearly requires our putting off the mind of the natural man, which is a carnal and sensual mind. Dismissing unclean things and also replacing them with clean actions—like worshiping the Lord, and doing good to others—reflects the keeping of the first and second great commandments. The natural man has no such inclinations to hinder his selfish acting out.

We are told in connection with the beguilement of Eve that Satan "knew not the mind of God" (Moses 4:6). How so, when he is otherwise so bright and clever? Besides, he has been around for so long too! One major reason for that cosmic ignorance is that the adversary is both unmeek and is a promoter of that which is unclean! Let us, therefore, strive for "the mind of Christ," by thinking more and more *as* He thinks but also by thinking *of what* He thinks.

The rewards of cleanliness are many, including receiving its own clear and sustaining witness of its efficacy. In that same master revelation, exhorting us to "let virtue garnish [our] thoughts unceasingly," is the promise "then shall [our] confidence wax strong in the presence of God." We could not have confidence in the Lord's presence or, meanwhile, "*always* have His Spirit to be with us" (as is regularly prayed for in the sacramental prayer on the bread), without having clean minds. Such are needed to make us feel genuinely at home in His kingdom and confident in His house. Then and only then can we have the Holy Ghost as our "constant companion," not merely as an occasional influence.

Furthermore, our purity also hastens our submissiveness to Jesus. Therefore, in our diverse, and sometimes trying, individual circumstances, if we are basically pure and we submissively acknowledge His hand in our lives *now*, we will feel the clasp of His welcoming arms *later* at the entrance to His kingdom, when our confidence will truly wax strong in the presence of God—for the caveat reminds that "no unclean thing can dwell with God" (1 Nephi 10:21).

It is not surprising that today's surrounding secularism has firmly partnered with relativism in an alliance of dalliance. Secularism sincerely practices what it preaches. Centuries ago there occurred an episode which parallels some of the secular trendiness in our own time. Opinion leaders back then proclaimed:

> . . . there could be no atonement made for the sins of men, but every man fared in this life according to the management of the creature; therefore every man prospered according to his genius, and that every man conquered according to his strength; and whatsoever a man did was no crime.
>
> And thus he did preach unto them, leading away the hearts of many, causing them to lift up their heads in their wickedness, yea, leading away many women, and also men, to commit whoredoms—telling them that when a man was dead, that was the end thereof. (Alma 30:17-18.)

Such is ethical relativism at the end of its journey, and it is similar in each era! Nothing is really wrong. Therefore, it is all right to conquer and prosper by one's strength and genius as we witness an indulgent individualism instead of real brotherhood.

Strange, isn't it, how once people stop believing in God they want to start playing God. Or is it? In any case, some so misread their circumstances because they do not see "things as they really are" (Jacob 4:13).

Illustrative of poor perspective of another type is the fact that, after jealously slaying Abel, Cain cried out in a pathetic outburst of self-deception, "I am free," but he was never less so! (Moses 5:33.) Like Pilate's trying to wash his hands in vain, and like Hitler's careful efforts to keep his name off certain Holocaust documents, so today many do not really want the consequences of what they want. But in God's inexorable ecology consequences do come, accompanied by severe individual accountability. Steep costs are levied on a declining people!

Being kept increasingly from error also facilitates our access to that great blessing of hope, something not available if we continue to be saturated in sin. This kind of hope means much more than our everyday usage of the word *hope* in which we "hope" to arrive at a certain destination by a certain time. We "hope" the world economy will improve. We "hope" for the visit of a loved one. Such typify our sincere but proximate hopes. No wonder life's disappointments make up so much of the debris of our proximate hopes.

Ultimate hope, however, is a very different matter. It is tied to Jesus and the blessings of the great Atonement, blessings resulting in the universal resurrection and the precious opportunity thereby provided for us to practice emancipating repentance, realizing eventually what the scriptures call "a perfect brightness of hope" (2 Nephi 31:20).

Mormon confirmed, "What is it that ye shall hope for? Behold I say unto you that ye shall have hope through the atonement of Christ." (Moroni 7:40-41; see also Alma 27:28.) Real hope, therefore, is not associated with things mercurial, but rather with things immortal and eternal!

Again it does not surprise us that hope is intertwined with other gospel doctrines, especially faith and patience. Just as doubt, despair, and desensitization go together, so do faith, hope, charity, and patience. The "bottom line" of Mormon's marvelous sermon is "charity." Charity, he teaches, is a manifestation of our inner meekness. And meekness sustains faith and hope. (See Moroni 7:43-45.)

These latter four qualities must be carefully and constantly nurtured by preeminent charity, however, whereas doubt and despair, like dandelions, need little encouragement in order to sprout and spread. Alas, despair comes so naturally to the natural man unconnected with the great realities of the universe! This includes what Arthur Henry King has called "the sobbing of a deserted soul" (*Arm the Children: Faith's Response to a Violent World* [Provo, Utah: BYU Studies, Brigham Young University, 1998], p. 238).

Faith and hope are constantly interactive and are not always easily or precisely distinguished. Nevertheless, ultimate hope's expectations are "with surety" true. (Ether 12:4; see also Romans 8:24; Hebrews 11:1; Alma 32:21.) Yet, in the geometry of the restored theology, hope corresponds to faith but sometimes has a greater circumference. Faith, in turn, constitutes "the assurance of things hoped for" and the proof of "things not seen" (JST, Hebrews 11:1; see also Ether 12:6). Thus hope sometimes reconnoiters beyond the present boundaries of faith, but it always radiates from faith in Jesus.

No wonder souls can be stirred and rallied by real hope's "reveille" as by no other music. Even if a few comrades slumber or desert, "lively hope" is still there "smiling brightly before us" ("We Thank Thee, O God, for a

Prophet," *Hymns*, no. 19; see 1 Peter 1:3). Hope caused downcast disciples to go quickly and expectantly to an empty garden tomb (see Mark 16:1-8; Luke 24:8-12). Hope helped a prophet to see rescuing rain in a distant cloud that appeared to be no larger than a man's hand (see 1 Kings 18:41-46).

Such ultimate hope constitutes the "anchor of the soul" and is retained through the gift of the Holy Ghost and faith in Christ (Hebrews 6:19; see also Alma 25:16; Ether 12:9). In contrast, viewing life without the prospect of immortality can diminish not only hope but also the sense of personal accountability (see 1 Corinthians. 6:19; Alma 30:18).

When hope is stripped away, however, Paul notes the tendency for some to eat and drink cavalierly, reasoning that "for to morrow we die," some no doubt driven by the erroneous conclusion that "when a man [is] dead, that [is] the end thereof" (1 Corinthians 15:32; Alma 30:18).

Real hope, instead, keeps us "anxiously engaged" in good causes even when these appear to be losing causes on the mortal scoreboard (see D&C 58:27). Likewise, real hope is much more than wishful musing. It stiffens, not slackens, the spiritual spine. Hope is serene, not giddy, eager without being naive, and pleasantly steady without being smug. Hope is realistic anticipation that takes the form of a determination—not only to survive adversity but, moreover, to "endure . . . well" to the end (D&C 121:8).

Though otherwise a "lively" attribute, hope stands quietly with us at funerals. Our tears are just as wet, but not because of despair. Rather, they are tears of heightened appreciation evoked by poignant separation. Those tears of separation change, erelong, becoming tears of glorious anticipation.

Genuine, ultimate hope helps us to be more loving even while the love of many others waxes cold (Matthew 24:12). We are to be more holy, even as the world ripens in iniquity; more courteous and patient in a rage-filled, coarsening, and curt world; and to be strong of heart even when the hearts of others fail them (see Moroni 10:22). By so striving, we will have more reason to praise the Giver of these gifts.

Hope can be contagious, especially if we are to be "ready always to give an answer to every man that asketh . . . a reason of the hope that is in [us]" (1 Peter 3:15).

Said President Brigham Young, if we do not so impart knowledge to others and do good, we "will become contracted" in our views and feelings (*Discourses of Brigham Young*, sel. John A. Widtsoe [Salt Lake City: Deseret Book Co., 1941], p. 335). Therefore, we should pray earnestly to God, "Help us now to serve Thee," amid the challenges of using our moral agency wisely, as we strive to become more error free.

Chapter Six

"In a Pleasing Way"

Among the especially powerful, restored doctrines of the kingdom, and one worthy of much more of our pondering and praise, is God's deep commitment to our moral agency. Its place in His plan is fundamental, especially in the face of restored truths that bring a knowledge of key things, past, present, and future. Such restored truths include "things as they really are, and . . . will be" (Jacob 4:13).

The verse to follow bears upon many fundamental things: "All truth is independent in that sphere in which God has placed it, to act for itself, as all intelligence[1] also; *otherwise there is no existence*" (D&C 93:30; emphasis added). Furthermore, the scriptures declare without elaboration: "Here is the agency of man" (verse 31).

---

[1] A caveat, however: we should make a distinction between scriptures that describe intelligence as "the light of truth," and intelligence as a noun that describes the eternal matter that constitutes the core of our existence.

Elder Stephen L Richards declared of this glorious truth of the Restoration:

> I set forth as the first aspect of this new interpretation the doctrine of the dominance of intelligence. I believe I am correct in the assertion that in all Christian literature prior to the advent of our Church there were to be found no such concepts of the origin, function, and place of intelligence in the universe as come from our modern scripture. Here are some excerpts:
>
>> Intelligence or the light of truth was not created or made, neither indeed can be.
>> All truth is independent in that sphere in which God has placed it, to act for itself, as all intelligence also. Otherwise, there is no existence. (Doctrine and Covenants 93:29, 30.)
>> The glory of God is intelligence—or in other words, light and truth.
>> Light and truth forsake that evil one. (Doctrine and Covenants 93:36, 37.)
>> Whatever principle of intelligence we attain unto in this life, it will rise with us in the resurrection.
>> And if a person gains more knowledge and intelligence in this life through his diligence and obedience than another, he will have so much the advantage in the world to come. (Doctrine and Covenants 130:18, 19.)

Now, since intelligence is co-eternal with God and is the very glory of God, it follows logically that it is the chief investiture of man. Indeed, it is man, for it is that part of his constituency that persists, that is eternal. This knowing, conceiving, illuminating principle of existence lies at the base of all our powers and potentialities. Without it there would be no virtue and no sin. It alone gives to man his free agency, the power to choose, to will, and to act, conscious of the effects of his decisions and his deeds. (In Conference Report, April 1938, p. 22.)

Writing on this same, vital subject, President Joseph Fielding Smith, then of the Twelve, added:

Some of our writers have endeavored to explain what an intelligence is, but to do so is futile, for we have never been given any insight into this matter beyond what the Lord has fragmentarily revealed. We know, however, that there is something called intelligence which always existed. It is the real eternal part of man, which was not created or made. This intelligence combined with the spirit constitutes a spiritual identity or individual. (*The Progress of Man* [Salt Lake City: Genealogical Society of Utah, 1936], p. 11.)

Therefore, since some things are yet unrevealed, we do not know with any precision exactly what was "brought with us" as, later on, we became spirit sons and daughters of our Father in Heaven. It is clear, however, that God did not fashion us *ex nihilo*, out of nothing. Our intrinsic makeup is not somehow all His responsibility; there is no "easy out" as to our individual accountability in the true gospel of Jesus Christ.

President Marion G. Romney, then in the Twelve, said

of our freedom to choose, "Abridge man's agency, and the whole purpose of his mortality is thwarted. Without it, the Lord says, there is no existence." (In Conference Report, April 1966, p. 99.)

Indeed, without the existence of choices, without our freedom to choose and without opposition, there would be no real existence. This is so much like Lehi's metaphor of how, in the absence of agency and opposites, things would have resulted in a meaningless, undifferentiated "compound in one" (2 Nephi 2:11). In such a situation the earth would actually have "no purpose in the end of its creation" (2 Nephi 2:12). It is a fact that we can neither grow spiritually nor thereby be truly happy unless and until we make wise use of our moral agency. Yet God will not "force the human mind" even in order to cause us to serve and worship Him. (See D&C 29:36.)

Instead, as between good or evil (even with all of their profound and attendant consequences), the scriptures emphasize: "Nevertheless, thou mayest choose for thyself" (JST, Genesis 2:21; Moses 3:17). Of this fundamental reality the Lord has said, "Behold, here is the agency of man, and here is the condemnation of man; because that which was from the beginning is plainly manifest unto them, and they receive not the light" (D&C 93:31). Father Lehi gave further expression, saying: "Because that they are redeemed from the fall they have become free forever, knowing good from evil; to act for themselves and not to be acted upon" (2 Nephi 2:26). Clearly, Jesus' declaration about how the truth can make us free is part of this spiritual equation (see John 8:32).

As with other key, doctrinal scriptures, those verses

associated with moral agency are densely packed with meaning at several different levels. Such is surely the case with Lehi's great sermon on agency. Therein he speaks of man's need to choose amid the reality that "it must needs be, that there is an opposition in all things" (2 Nephi 2:11). Lehi tells us that this principle operated "even [in] the forbidden fruit" (2 Nephi 2:15). Elder Jeffrey R. Holland has described life's ongoing "opposition" as presenting us with "contending enticements" (*Christ and the New Covenant* [Salt Lake City: Deseret Book Co., 1997], p. 202).

This "competition" is real, but without such alternatives our agency would be meaningless. In fact, without agency there could be no felicity or happiness. Hence, man really remains "free to choose liberty and eternal life . . . or . . . captivity and death" (2 Nephi 2:27). Thus the availability of "contending enticements" is necessary in order that man can truly act for himself, while being "enticed by the one or the other" (2 Nephi 2:16).

Granted, we usually think of enticements as being associated with evil, but there can be enticing desires for righteousness, too. Therefore, King Benjamin pleads for us to follow "the enticings of the Holy Spirit" (Mosiah 3:19). Of course, the adversary has totally different motives when he entices us, striving to have us become "miserable like unto himself" (2 Nephi 2:27).

Without any real choices and without the capacity for differentiation along with "opposition," things would form, just as Lehi said, an undifferentiated "compound in one" (2 Nephi 2:11). If this had been the result, the earth would have "no purpose in the end of its creation" (2 Nephi 2:12); there would be no real existence (see D&C 93:30).

Perhaps the imagery of a "compound in one" is intended to connote a hypothetical blending that loses any distinctiveness. In any case, the scriptural phrase "compound in one," with its litany of opposites, makes clear all that would thereby be lost; we would get nothing! In effect, things would "remain as dead" (2 Nephi 2:11).

So there is a clear friction between agency and opposition, but it is a necessary friction, if we are to progress. Hence knowing the truth about divine standards and then choosing aright is essential to our growth and happiness and freedom, but we will feel the friction! Moreover, if things were in a "compound in one," we could not learn from our mortal experiences, because we would not experience the opposites. Furthermore, we could not be held accountable either, because no real and clear choices would be before us, given the "compound" circumstance. Individuality would be inert!

In the family tree of doctrines pertaining to the plan of salvation, therefore, moral agency is root and branch. If things had formed a "compound in one," as Lehi further declared, we could not really "act for [ourselves]" but we would inertly be "acted upon."

It is ironic that those who wrongly choose to celebrate their capacity to feel grossly—slavish sensation seekers—eventually become "past feeling" anyway, producing an outcome of insensibility; the very outcome so much to be avoided in Father's plan (1 Nephi 17:45; Moroni 9:20; 2 Nephi 2:11). Yet some end up doing indirectly what the Lord's plan forbade directly!

Without the plan's saving arrangement there could be no righteousness, no wickedness, no holiness, no misery, no good, and no bad. Indeed, there could be no plan of happiness, because full happiness depends upon our deliberate choosing of individual righteousness. This primacy of agency in the plan "answer[s] the ends of the atonement," which mercifully permits us to choose to repent (2 Nephi 2:10). In God's plan, formed before the world was, the terms of specific punishment are "affixed," and likewise are the conditions of happiness (2 Nephi 2:10; Alma 42:18, 22).

As BYU professor David Paulsen has thoughtfully written of the mortal experience: "Without moral righteousness, there is no happiness; without significant moral freedom, there is no moral righteousness; without an opposition (opposing possibilities to choose between), there is no significant moral freedom. Thus, happiness and opposition are essentially related." (November 1994 letter.)

Since it is only out of righteous choices that character and happiness come, Samuel, the Lamanite, speaks of the futility of happiness being sought by "doing iniquity." He declares such an approach is not only spiritually wrong but also intellectually naive, being "contrary to the nature of that righteousness which is in our great and Eternal Head." (Helaman 13:38.) Therefore, happiness is actually not obtainable in doing iniquity any more than it is obtainable without agency. In fact, the "carnal state" is one in which some individuals live "without God in the world"; they have, alas, gone "contrary to the nature of God; therefore, they are in a state contrary to the nature of happiness" (Alma 41:11).

The "nature of happiness" requires us to know about "things as they really are, and . . . things as they really will be" (Jacob 4:13). To be ignorant of the soaring realities of God's plan is, in one degree or another, to "live without God in the world," which lifestyle is so desensitizing and depriving (Ephesians 2:12; Mosiah 27:31). No wonder the scriptures, instead, speak of our need to become "alive in Christ" (2 Nephi 25:25).

As to our so savoring of life, several scriptures use the word *taste*, as when some did "taste of . . . exceeding joy" (Alma 36:24). Other and almost exclamatory words appear elsewhere involving both taste and sight:

> And it came to pass that I did go forth and partake of the fruit thereof; and I beheld that it was most sweet, above all that I ever before tasted. Yea, and I beheld that the fruit thereof was white, to exceed all the whiteness that I had ever seen. (1 Nephi 8:11.)

Alma even blends the senses, speaking of having "tasted" light, meaning to have "experienced" light (Alma 32:35). Mormon speaks of having "tasted . . . of the goodness of Jesus" (Mormon 1:15; Alma 36:26). "Taste," in the spiritual sense, involves the capacity to savor joy, sweetness, goodness, and light, for they are "discernible." But such would simply not be possible if things were in a "compound in one." (Alma 32:35; 2 Nephi 2:11.)

Even so, we are not only to possess the capacity to discern and distinguish thusly; we are also to use our agency so that we come to prefer, and even strongly desire, the taste of gospel goodness, sweetness, and joy. This is part of educating the tastebuds of the soul. And we happily note that what is discernible by one individual is also verifiable in the very same ways by another, as is well described in Alma chapter 32.

Thus the correct use of agency empowers as well as enlivens us spiritually! In contrast, how does one "taste" or draw nourishment from a tasteless "compound in one"?

Furthermore, only those who have significantly developed the tastebuds of the soul will be even partially prepared for the incredible beauties of the world ahead, one in which "eye hath not seen, nor ear heard, . . . the things which God hath prepared for them that love him" (1 Corinthians 2:9).

Meanwhile, so many fail to connect the joyless sameness of sinners that results in the very joyless insensibility spoken of by Father Lehi. In contrast, the more saintly become ever more tastefully discerning and sensitive; they are filled with more joy. In fact, the very concept of a "compound in one" rejects the discerning differentiation made possible by increasing saintliness.

For instance, if in daily life we assault our ears with sounds that are not truly music, we may lose our capacity to distinguish beautiful music from mere noise, another type of "compound in one." One note does not a symphony make![2]

---

[2] Brigham Young observed that "there is no music in hell" (*Discourses of Brigham Young*, sel. John A. Widtsoe [Salt Lake City: Deseret Book Co., 1941], p. 242). Doubtless a correct statement as to real music! But some contemporary sounds, masquerading as music, belong quite naturally to that grim place, where their presence would further entitle that awful place to be called *hell!*

So it is that the wise use of agency is linked not only with accountability but also with beauty and felicity. Without developing that distinguishing capacity that goes with wisely used agency, we would be like the undiscerning who anciently heard "the voice of God," but thought it was merely thunder (John 12:29). How sad not to even recognize His voice, let alone not to hear what God had to say! Clearly those who "know not the mind of God" have not only failed to develop the "mind of Christ" but they also lack the ears to hear! (See 1 Corinthians 2:16.)

In the mortal process of choosing, we ourselves determine what our own prevailing desires are. No wonder, therefore, President Joseph F. Smith spoke about the need for us to engage in "the education of our desires" (see *Gospel Doctrine* [Salt Lake City: Deseret Book Co., 1939], p. 297). In the use of our agency we are fundamentally sovereign. Given the constant and basic role of our desires, a significant portion of real discipleship consists of the "education of our desires." If we are meek, our capacity to learn from our experiences will reflect how we educate our desires, even in the hard experiences. After all, it is we, individually, who shape our desires and determine to which of the "contending enticements" we will finally respond and from which we will experience happiness, if we choose aright.

Thus, given God's plan and agency's vital role in it, we must ever be on guard against today's trends and patterns, however carefully they are camouflaged, in which operative agency is severely diminished, such as when some seek to avoid or to deny personal accountability or to say there are really no fixed values. Ethical relativism can thereby lead to a type of a "compound in one" by an undifferentiated life or simply by ruling out moral absolutes and thereby encouraging every man to walk in his own way (D&C 1:16; see also Judges 21:25; 2:10).

There is a deep irony in the sameness of sinners who think they are individualistic. They have given away, at least temporarily, their agency and their capacity for joy, living life on a single plane; or, more descriptive still, some march like lemmings down the slope to the gulf of misery.

The ultimate consequences will be real and harsh, because

> that which breaketh a law, and abideth not by law, but seeketh to become a law unto itself, and willeth to abide in sin, and altogether abideth in sin, cannot be sanctified by law, neither by mercy, justice, nor judgment. Therefore, they must remain filthy still. (D&C 88:35.)

A powerful magnetism is thus quietly at work in what at first may seem to be mere philosophical differences. Nevertheless, these result in converging and sad consequences: "And if ye shall say there is no law, ye shall also say there is no sin" (2 Nephi 2:13). Those who deny the existence of any absolutes in their own ways fulfill this scripture, as situational ethics prevail.

Yet with all that has just been said, it is easy for us to agree to the vital role of agency in the abstract but much harder to be fully appreciative of agency in the rough and tumble of life. For example, some struggle and even despair over the human consequences of misused agency, because of the global and individual suffering it causes. Some even try to push away all they can of the burdens of choosing, giving away all of the proxies they can. Some demand as evidence of His existence that God intervene to stop the terrible consequences of our bad choices.

Once again, the wisdom of President Joseph F. Smith comes to the fore. He observed of human suffering that nevertheless God "permits" choices to be made by humans of which He clearly doesn't approve (see *Improvement Era* 20 [July 1917]: 821).

Besides, without an "opposition in all things," where are the isometrics required for individual development, such as when the new self is pitted against the old? Consider this simple illustration by scientist Alan Hayward of behavior when forced by "compulsory means":

Suppose for a moment that God made His presence felt all the time—that every action of ours, good or bad, brought an immediate response from Him in the form of reward or punishment. What sort of a world would this be then?

It would resemble, on a grander scale, the dining room of a hotel . . . where I once stayed for a few days. The European owner evidently did not trust his . . . waiters. He would sit on a raised platform at one end of the room, constantly watching every movement. Goods that might possibly be pilfered, such as tea bags, sugar knobs and even pats of butter or margarine, were doled out by him in quantities just sufficient for the needs of the moment. He would scrutinize every bill like Sherlock Holmes looking for signs of foul play.

The results of all this supervision were painfully obvious. I have stayed in many hotels around the world . . . but never have I met such an unpleasant bunch of waiters as in that hotel. Their master's total lack of trust in them had warped their personalities. As long as he was watching they acted discreetly, but the moment they thought his guard was down they would seize the opportunity to misbehave.

In much the same way, it would ruin our own characters if God's presence were as obvious as that of the [hotel owner]. This would then be a world without trust, without faith, without unselfishness, without love—a world where everybody obeyed God because it paid them to do so. Horrors! (*God Is* [New York: Thomas Nelson, 1978], p. 134.)

If instead, speaking hypothetically, the Lord were to show His power constantly, as some mortals wrongfully wish Him to do, our lot would be one of prompt punishment rather than divine love and long-suffering. God would then silence all opposition, but He would not be an all-loving God. He would have destroyed His own plan of happiness! Such enforced cooperation would not produce a society of illuminated individuality but, rather, an indistinguishable "compound in one" (2 Nephi 2:11). We would then have an enforced and an undifferentiated "salvation," an outcome rejected so long ago (Moses 4:1). People might even think they were "saved," just as murdering Cain thought he was "free"!

No wonder that for a host of reasons Satan seeks to "destroy the agency of man"! (Moses 4:3.)

While God has yet to tell us all the implications, if things were to be in a "compound in one" we can be certain that in such blobbishness and lumpiness there would be no prospect that "men . . . might have joy" (2 Nephi 2:25).

Meanwhile, therefore, we are left to "do according to [our] own will" (Mosiah 2:21), so "that every man may act in doctrine and principle pertaining to futurity, according to the moral agency which I have given unto him, that every man may be accountable for his own sins in the day of judgment" (D&C 101:78). Hence fairness, as well as happiness, is deeply involved!

Elder Jeffrey R. Holland has observed insightfully that "the word *probation* is found only ten times in the Standard Works, and nine of those references are in the Book of Mormon" (*Christ and the New Covenant*, p. 209). We can't get very far in understanding life and God's purposes without our understanding this "probation" portion of God's plan of happiness. Advocacy and judging by Jesus are thus implicit! Probation is clearly linked to our using mortal time well by becoming wisely experienced in the use of our agency. Clearly these immense truths about agency are among the "plain and precious things" restored (see 1 Nephi 13:26-29).

Each mortal, at least initially, has "the light of Christ" to guide (Alma 29:14; Moroni 7:19; D&C 88:7). This light can prompt us, if we will, in the wise use of our agency. If, however, it is extinguished or severely diminished, we are at risk. Thus, to help us with our agency, God gives us our consciences and, for some, the great gift of the Holy Ghost. Furthermore, God is long-suffering and redemptive as He works with us. But we are personally and finally accountable for our wrong choices, which, alas, bring misery not only to ourselves, but to others as well.

Thus, in His plan of happiness the love of God meets the agency of man in so many ways. These touching points we cannot now fully diagram; we cannot yet connect all the dots all of the time! But the outline is clearly there!

The comforting key to dealing with our mistakes is Jesus' great atonement, by means of which, if we repent, we can achieve the needed reconciliation and emancipation. Even though we may not now fully comprehend the marvelous and glorious atonement, we can, nevertheless, experience it in goodly measure. We can do this while simultaneously educating our desires and experiencing and succeeding against opposition, as we strive "to apply the atoning blood of Christ" (Mosiah 4:2).

In any case, the deeper our understanding of the role of agency becomes, the deeper our gratitude will be for it, including our much greater appreciation for the tremendous and redeeming restraint exercised by our loving Father as He watches His erring children.

Of course our individual patterns of genes, circumstances, and environments matter very much, for these do impinge upon us and do shape us and our choices significantly. Yet there remains an inner zone in which we are accountably sovereign. In this zone lies the essence of our individuality. Furthermore, we have been developing, as ourselves, for a long, long time. Though we do not have all the revealed details, the intimations are there in the revelations and are also there in such instructive words as these from President Joseph Fielding Smith:

If the Lord declares that intelligence, something which we do not fully understand, was co-eternal with him and always existed, there is no argument that we can or should present to contradict it. Why he cannot create intelligence is simply because intelligence, like time and space, always existed. (*Answers to Gospel Questions*, 5 vols. [Salt Lake City: Deseret Book Co. 1957–66], 3:125.)

In fact, we were with God in the beginning (D&C 93:29). In contrast, there is the widely held concept of an "out of nothing" creation—with all of its agency-reducing implications. This errant teaching confronts its adherents with a severe dilemma about human suffering and about God's character, as pointedly put by one commentator:

We cannot say that [God] would like to help but cannot: God is omnipotent. We cannot say that he would help if he only knew: God is omniscient. We cannot say that he is not responsible for the wickedness of others: God creates those others. Indeed an omnipotent, omniscient God [who creates all things absolutely—i.e., out of nothing] must be an accessory before (and during) the fact to every human misdeed; as well as being responsible for every non-moral defect in the universe. (Antony Flew, "Theology and Falsification," in *New Essays in Philosophical Theology*, ed. Antony Flew and Alasdair MacIntyre [New York: Macmillan, 1955], p. 107.)

No wonder it is so vital to understand God's soaring character and his felicitous purposes by better understanding our agency! George MacDonald observed of the contracted view of God held by so many, "I suspect a great part of our irreligion springs from our disbelief in the humanity of God" (*The Miracles of Our Lord* [London: Strahan and Co., 1870], p. 265). Beliefs do have consequences. Failure to understand both the character and the purposes of God can lessen the religious feelings of individuals!

In fact, while God has given us so many enabling gifts in addition to the gift of life, the only real gift we can actually give Him is to submit our will to His (Mosiah 15:7; 3:19). Therefore, if a plan opposite to the Lord's plan had prevailed, it would not only have abrogated our agency; it would also have prevented us from giving God the one precious gift, our wills! It is the only one we can really give to Him that is not already His!

In the final judgment we will receive what we deserve; but meanwhile, God will not "force the human mind" in order for us to receive what could have been otherwise.

Hence one's misused agency can inexorably create a pattern of choices pointed towards misery instead of felicity. Even the first tiny droplets of decision suggest a direction. Then the little inflecting rivulets come, merging into small brooks, and soon into larger streams; finally one is swept along by a vast river which finally flows into the "gulf of misery and endless wo" (Helaman 5:12).

The choice of outcome is always up to us. Therein lies life's greatest and most persistent challenge: as to our pattern of choices, in which direction do we face?

If we are wise, we will use our daily mortal experience in ways in which "all these things shall give [us] experience and shall be for [our] good" (D&C 122:7).

Brigham Young spoke emphatically about how all of life's daily moments are to be wisely used, however ordinary these moments may seem to be:

It is the aggregate of the acts which I perform through life that makes up the conduct that will be exhibited in the day of judgment, and when the books are opened, there will be the life which I have lived for me to look upon, and there also will be the acts of your lives for you to look upon. Do you not know that the building up of the kingdom of God, the gathering of Israel, is to be done by little acts? You breathe one breath at a time; each moment is set apart to its act, and each act to its moment. It is the moments and the little acts that make the sum of the life of man. Let every second, minute, hour, and day we live be spent in doing that which we know to be right. (In *Journal of Discourses* 3:342.)

Hence for serious disciples who would act "in a pleasing way," there are no ordinary people, but likewise there are really no ordinary moments! Moment by moment we are shaped by our choices—large and small. The daily quizzes matter along with the major exams.

Indeed, as to the daily use of our agency, we should daily plead, "Father, help us now to serve Thee in a pleasing way"—especially in the face of our "unnumbered blessings."

Praise him for his mer - cy; Praise him for his love.

For un-num-bered bless - ings Praise the Lord a - bove.

Let our hap-py voic - es Still the notes pro - long.

One a - lone is wor - thy Of our sweet-est song.

CHAPTER SEVEN

"For Unnumbered Blessings"

So often, among so many other praiseworthy blessings, life features the intertwinings of our lives which we can scarcely number. Yet why should we be surprised? Do we not sometimes use phrases such as "instant friends" and "kindred spirits"? After all, those within our individual circles of influence definitely constitute our particular portion of humanity—those whom God expects us in particular to love and to serve. Within our intersecting circles, whatever their size and extent, lie many unused opportunities for service, "enough and to spare" (D&C 104:17). These intersectings mercifully provide multiple opportunities, and they can bring "unnumbered blessings."

As close associates can readily testify, I have long since entered my "anecdotage," yet I hope this chapter is more than that. In noting several examples of my own intertwinings, while hoping memory does not unintentionally distort, my sole purpose is to express humble gratitude by means of this small sample of recollections; these remembrances that bless me even today. These recollections reflect instructions and important tutorings.

As a boy I lived in Salt Lake City near Nibley Park golf course, where very occasionally I saw President Heber J. Grant play. When erring golfers would sometimes hit balls over the fence, we boys would scamper to bring them back. If lucky, we would usually get a nickel in return. Unfortunately, at least for us boys, President Heber J. Grant tended to go straight down the fairway; he rarely hit any balls over the fence. But one time when he did, he gave a quarter to the lucky retriever!

As I saw President Grant playing golf, I could not know then that I would be blessed, about fifty years later, to sit in the same upper room of the temple where he sat for so many decades and even presided. In that same room President Grant's portrait, along with those of all the other past and present presidents, continues to look down each Thursday upon today's assembled First Presidency and Twelve and upon periodic meetings for all the General Authorities. I have thought several times of seeing President Grant play golf and of that generous quarter. I have reflected even more on President Grant's much more important gift to all of us of a long and prophetic span of leadership. Yet this span was preceded by his hard, tutoring apostolic years in Japan, where his diligent missionary work seemed so unproductive at the time.

While I was living later in East Mill Creek as a boy, a friend of mine and I would occasionally ride his horse over to the low-lying hills surrounding the Country Club golf course. We would find a few lost, but relatively new, golf balls on the hillsides and sell them to passing foursomes, all of whom seemed to the two of us, back then, to be very rich. Foreshadowing intertwinings to come, one such business foursome included banker Orval W. Adams, who once generously bought two thirsty and sweaty boys a soda pop. Later came other unforeseen intertwinings. In about ten years' time I was to serve in the Canadian Mission with Orval's youngest son, Web, a friend then and ever since. Thirty years after the soda pop, I was named to, but could scarcely fill, the place on the board of directors of Mountain Fuel Supply just vacated by financier Orval Adams. Today Orval Adams's great-grandson, Jeff, and his great-granddaughter, Christina, live in our ward. It is interesting that these two fine children also stand in that same relationship to President David O. McKay.

Life is best measured not in days but in defining moments, not in weeks but in works. My defining moments—like yours—have often been unexpected, uninvited, and were often unappreciated at the time. One such moment occurred when (at about age sixteen) I was coasting lazily along academically. An English teacher at Granite High School, Mary Mason, gave me a low grade, a D. It was, she said, a jolt to stimulate me. She thereby quickened my interest in English, though too late to get a decent final grade from her. Though I wish I could sit anew with Mary Mason to thank her, I was privileged to thank her several times, years later, and to bless Miss Mason when, after her retirement, she was ill with cancer. Still later, I was privileged to praise her at her funeral.

I again publicly express my gratitude for Miss Mason's discipline and teaching, including how to diagram sentences. She helped my sense of grammar which, in turn, helped me to communicate at least somewhat better the grammar of the gospel while writing some twenty-five books. Even so, I could still use Mary Mason's crisp editing, and, significantly, I still crave her approval.

Correction can be such a blessing in life! Sometimes, however, it comes as a very well-disguised blessing.

As with many of you, I was born "of goodly parents," which provided a series of defining moments. What was immediately ingested in that home was not fully digested until much later. For instance, several times, though unheard by them, I remember hearing vocal, parental prayers in which my sisters and I were pled for by name. My father's patriarchal blessing said his voice would often be "raised in mighty prayer." It was, and I and my sisters were both witnesses and beneficiaries.

I remember, too, watching that convert father, as a ward clerk, carefully counting tithing and offerings on our round dining table after a fast day. Silver dollars and even pennies were carefully stacked and counted. It seemed like so much money, especially when we, along with everyone else living around us, were poor together, but we didn't know it. But these were *sacred* funds. I did not doubt my father knew it! Besides, in that imperfect but humble home, we were nevertheless rich in the things that really mattered.

Like our fathers and mothers, you and I, as parents and grandparents, do some of our best teaching when we are unaware of observing eyes and listening ears.

I vividly remember seeing my six-week-old sister, Carol, near death with whooping cough when no antibiotics were available. At crisis point, when she appeared to me to have stopped breathing, she was placed on that same round dining table and was quickly blessed to survive by my father and a neighbor high priest. I thus witnessed, firsthand, the power of the priesthood. By the way, this pivotal experience occurred well before I'd read and received my own witness of the Book of Mormon or knew of so many other key things in the Restoration. We learn line upon line, and experience by experience.

Belief can grow into faith in each of us. Faith can become personal knowledge. Usually it happens incrementally, however, just as Alma taught (see Alma 32). Validation thus occurs episodically and personally, experiment by experiment and experience by experience. In this way, we come to know a particular truth "in that thing," and then "[our minds] begin to expand" (Alma 32:34).

Our home was one in which there was a lively, parental interest in gospel doctrines, especially as parents prepared various lessons for their classes. Though otherwise quite shy, in his enthusiasm Dad even used to write, way back then, occasional letters of gospel inquiry to Church leaders such as then Elder Joseph Fielding Smith and President David O. McKay and later to Elder Bruce McConkie. He would let me read the inquiring letters and the kind and patient answers. It is no surprise that more intertwinings and touching points were to occur subsequently, such as being privileged to introduce a by then unsteady, but warm, President McKay to the eminent historian Arnold Toynbee. President McKay's quick, scriptural quip concerning his slight swaying, because of very advanced age, was, "I stagger, but not with strong drink" (Isaiah 29:9).

Years after his replies to Dad, President Joseph Fielding

Smith was in the head chair in the First Presidency's board-
room on the June morning in 1970 when I was called as
Church Commissioner of Education. Two special mentors,
President Harold B. Lee and President N. Eldon Tanner, sat
on President Smith's right and left, respectively.
Furthermore, in 1981 Elder Bruce R. McConkie welcomed
me especially warmly as a colleague in the Quorum of the
Twelve.

So many have mentored me and are so deserving of
mention. Of those now deceased, President Harold B. Lee,
President Spencer W. Kimball, President N. Eldon Tanner,
and President Marion G. Romney come quickly and firmly
to mind especially. I have praised President Gordon B.
Hinckley, President Thomas S. Monson, and President
James E. Faust more recently in a general conference
address.

For the purposes of this volume, however, I seek to
focus a few sentences on President Lee, who was so kind to
me over a decade of close association. His special tutoring
of me was accompanied by a special trusting of me. Since
he sensed my keen need for his wisdom and experience,
even his candor was a kindness. As a young Regional
Representative, I watched him select a stake president and
a patriarch in Malad, Idaho, which struck me then, as it
does now, as having been done by sheer revelation. He was
very warm and relaxed, but he was very clear about what
was to be done then.

President Lee seemed to me to be ever teaching. Would
that I had been ever learning! I felt his love as well as his
counsel, again and again.

His daughter, Helen Lee Goates, "adds her own personal witness and tribute to her spiritually powerful and loving father and her angelic mother."

. . . I realize that I had the ideal combination of parents: a father who was gentle beneath his firmness, and a mother who was firm beneath her gentleness. (L. Brent Goates, *Harold B. Lee: Prophet & Seer* [Salt Lake City: Bookcraft, 1985], p. 139.)

I feel privileged to have seen and experienced President Lee's gentleness a number of times. His son-in-law, Brent Goates, observed in his dedicatory, graveside prayer that President Lee had a pattern of being "early," such as coming into the Twelve at such an early age and being "early" in developing the modern welfare plan. His many and needed talents and gifts were "drafted" by the Lord, causing what seemed to us his "early" release as President of the Church.

For me, he was always there. When I was approached and was somewhat tempted over a quarter of a century ago to reach for the laurel wreath in politics, he was gentle and nondirective in his counsel, leaving the decision to me. Upon hearing my views, however, he seemed to be pleased with my declining such possibilities.

The periodic intersectings of our lives are marked, of course, by interruptions and resumptions. God clearly makes "multiple use" of these shared learning situations. What do these intertwinings signify? To be sure, God is in the details of each of our lives especially to the extent we allow. Hence, not only in the cosmos do "all things bear record of [the Lord]," but likewise in our lives, "all things denote there is a God." No wonder we are to confess His hand in all things. (Moses 6:63; Alma 30:44; D&C 59:21.)

Surprises and *coincidences* are the words we provincial mortals often use to describe such experiences. But these are scarcely appropriate words to describe the workings of an omniscient and loving God!

God has categorically assured us of His stunning capacity, saying, "I am able to do mine own work" (2 Nephi 27:20-21). Being omniscient, He sees the end from the beginning. Furthermore, He has made "ample provision" for all contingencies that result from the misuses of our moral agency and is still able to bring to pass His purposes. (See Joseph Smith, *Teachings of the Prophet Joseph Smith*, sel. Joseph Fielding Smith [Salt Lake City: Deseret Book Co., 1938], p. 220.) God's hand, somehow, is in things, including the intertwinings, yet without compromising our precious agency.

However, back to this small litany of remembrances. Sequentially, next came World War II, and, erelong, it was off to war! So many of us looked to Church leaders for certain assurances in those troubled and strange times. From the World War II serviceman's handbook I remember reading reassuringly:

When, therefore, constitutional law, obedient to these principles, calls the manhood of the Church into the armed service of any country to which they owe allegiance, their highest civic duty requires that they meet that call. If, harkening to that call and obeying those in command over them, they shall take the lives of those who fight against them, that will not make of them mur-

derers, nor subject them to the penalty that God has prescribed for those who kill, beyond the principle to be
mentioned shortly. For it would be a cruel God that would
punish His children as moral sinners for acts done by them
as the innocent instrumentalities of a sovereign whom He
had told them to obey and whose will they were powerless
to resist. (A message of the First Presidency dated April 6,
1942, in Gordon B. Hinckley, *A Brief Statement of
Principles of the Gospel.* . . . [Salt Lake City: The Church
of Jesus Christ of Latter-day Saints, 1943], p. 252.)

Involvement in World War II brought more intertwinings.

Unknown to me then was how the ravages of the battle
on Okinawa were affecting an eight-year-old Okinawan
boy, Kensei Nagamine. His father and brother were killed
in the Battle of Shuri, and his pregnant mother was able to
take her five children, including this youthful son, to the
north end of the island and comparative safety, even as
they were repeatedly machine-gunned by fighter planes
many times. Though unaware, an eighteen- and an eight-
year-old were then only miles apart. Many years later we
met; by then he was the president of the Okinawa Stake. It
was my privilege later on (after his tour as stake president)
to call him as patriarch to the Okinawa Stake. He is now
President Nagamine of the Tokyo temple! Surely the Lord
had His eyes upon him long ago! I have been greatly blessed
to come to know him and his missionary-minded family.

Among my Okinawa "buddies" is one nonmember for
whose grandson I was able to perform a recent sealing in
the Salt Lake Temple. These happy intertwinings seem to

go on and on, including very recently my being privileged to offer a prayer at the graveside service for my Catholic and foxhole buddy, Paul Montrone.

Having been trained and ordained at home, I blessed my sacrament several times in foxholes on Okinawa in May of 1945. As a reflex action I abstained from the coffee brought up to those of us "on the line." The army, in its typical inefficiency, sometimes did not bring up any water at all. However, my complying with the Word of Wisdom was no big deal. Yet thirty years later I learned that one foxhole buddy apparently had been watching this small act of compliance. As noted earlier, for us to be unaware does not mean we are unobserved.

The foxhole buddy, Chris Seil of California, did some observing. Over three decades later, the shared experience on Okinawa, though Chris was not a Church member, caused his member-wife, Barbara, to write a touching letter from California inquiring with these lines:

> I am a member of the Church, but my husband is a non member, however, he has supported our two sons on their missions. . . .
>
> In May or June of 1945 my husband was serving in the Army in the 77th Infantry Div. . . . During this two-week period my husband (Chris) shared fox holes with a Mormon boy who really lived his religion. The boy gave Chris all of his beer, coffee and cigarette rations in exchange for my husband's water. . . . The boy did not preach Mormonism to Chris, but he lived his religion as he should. My husband was not only grateful, but was really impressed with this boy, and loved and admired him, . . .

After this period . . . Each boy went his own way, and Chris doesn't ever remember seeing him again. . . .

I have heard the story of the Mormon boy many times during the years but no name was ever mentioned, . . .

The other night a strange thing happened. My husband and I were talking about the change in the U.S. Presidency. I mentioned that I hoped the new administration would not get us into another war as our boys would certainly be in it. My husband said, "That's right, the Mormons don't believe in being conscientious objectors do they?" Then he again told me the story of the Mormon boy and how hard he had fought even though he was very religious, and as Chris talked about it, he mentioned the boy's last name, and he was so startled that he said, "Quick, write that name down before I forget it." . . . [then] he had a very strong urge to get in touch with this man and express his appreciation to him personally.

The fellow's last name was Maxwell, and the only Maxwell I know in the Church is you, and I figured you would be a good person to start with.

We realize you are very busy, but perhaps you could give us some information: Are you that person?

A voice from the past which was to affect the future!

In further intertwinings I was blessed later to perform sealings for Chris and Barbara's sons. Barbara has been serving for several years as a worker in the Los Angeles Temple.

Once again, the joys of these intertwinings are so clear. Some day, in my opinion, we shall see that these intertwinings are not simply a function of mortality but went on before in our first estate, and surely they will continue in our third and final estate! If this is true, what seem to be friendships of initiation here are actually friendships of resumption.

Only about two years ago I learned from my aunt, Arlene Ash Turner, something precious of which I was completely unaware. It occurred back in May of 1945—the Okinawa period, where I was serving as a frightened infantryman in a mortar squad. Arlene told me that one day my mother had told her that the night before she and Dad had had their parental prayers and had prayed over me and my sisters. When abed they were nearly asleep, Mother reportedly said, "Clarence, we need to get out of bed and pray again. Neal is in grave danger!" They did, pleading for me afresh. I do not know the precise date, but the time zones are such that their late-night prayer would match mid-afternoon or early evening on Okinawa. The Japanese had been trying to hit our mortar squad position but were unable to do so because of some low, intervening hills. They must have moved their artillery pieces, because soon a round of artillery came squarely in between two of our foxholes. Shaken, I prayed most earnestly (doubtless along with others), naively promising to pay the Lord back. Relief came! Now, of course, I am much more in His debt.

I do not know the date of the parental prayer, but in the words of some other young men who had special mothers and who also went off to war, I "did not doubt [my mother] knew it" (see Alma 56:48).

Having such prayerful parents was a great inspiration to all of us in the family, and to learn so many years later of that simple but powerful act has been a great source of joy to me; and it has caused me to weep with appreciation more than once.

I had saved money during those twenty-plus months overseas in order to go on a mission, which was part of keeping my promise to the Lord made in May of 1945. When discharged, I wanted to go on a mission right away. But our bishop did not call me at once. Finally, somewhat audaciously, I went to his home one night and told him I wanted to go on a mission, had the money, and didn't want to wait. He then proceeded to process the call. I wondered back then why he seemed slow. Only decades later did I learn (from a good man who was then his ward clerk) that the bishop had felt, since I had been overseas for a while, I shouldn't be rushed into the mission field. Oh, how quick we are to judge, and sometimes with so little data!

Just prior to going into the mission field I was set apart as a full-time missionary for The Church of Jesus Christ of Latter-day Saints by Elder Matthew Cowley, whom I had never met before. During the course of the setting apart, Elder Cowley said, in effect, "Elder Maxwell, you are going to Eastern Canada to preach the gospel. Please stay out of political discussions." Those who know me know of my keen and long-standing interest in things political. Elder Cowley's counsel, therefore, was laser-like in its precision. He also gave me wise, precise, and personal counsel several years later when he performed the sealing for Colleen and me in the Salt Lake Temple for our eternal marriage. My two times with this Apostle gave clear evidence of his capacity to receive personal revelation for the benefit of those he blessed and counseled.

I was particularly blessed during the defining season, which the mission field surely constituted, with two wonderful mission presidents, President Octave W. Ursenbach and President Floyed G. Eyre, along with their special wives. Each of them tutored, loved, and taught me, though differently.

Upon my release, President Eyre, in his excellent script, inscribed a praise-filled "P.S." on his letter of my release to the Wandamere Ward bishop. A little praise can be such a large motivator. In a way, I have been running for fifty years on a postscript that was written in fifty seconds! If only you and I do not become too busy with so many earthly cares that we fail to give a little heavenly praise! I have never shared that letter except with Colleen and our children. In a recent intertwining, I have felt humbly grateful for the privilege of sealing several of President and Sister Eyre's grandchildren in the holy temple.

In 1947, our mission, by the way, had no study plan. Study plans in missions back then were rare and random. No wonder we didn't baptize as many as today. Out of my frustration, I developed a study plan which was very immodestly entitled, "The Sword of Truth." It was a good-faith effort but contained many typographical errors. Fortunately much better plans soon came along.

Later on, Colleen, who counseled me wisely as to my career path, encouraged me to accept an offer in 1956 of a job at the University of Utah after working for Senator Wallace F. Bennett in Washington, D.C. She said to me, insightfully: "I think you should work at the 'U.' Maybe you will have some influence on students." I scoffed gently. This didn't seem very likely to happen to an assistant director of Public Relations busily preparing news releases. But through the blessings of the Lord I ended up, over time, teaching hundreds of students political science, serving as a counselor in a bishopric to Oscar W. McConkie, Jr., then bishop of one of the first student wards, and served still later as Dean of Students.

I am blessed to have known and learned from many wonderful University students. Their lives keep intersecting with my own—all over the world! Now, sparked by several former students and generous friends, a professorial chair has been named in my honor at the "U." Its occupants can bless other generations of students! Colleen was "spot on," once again!

Though the foregoing samples are but few, I hope to be worthy not only of the individuals named but of all of my many friends, and especially of Him who "condescends" to call us His friends.

The blessings of our Heavenly Father to all of us are surely those of a very generous God. Even the much lesser telestial kingdom will be a place "which surpasses all understanding" (D&C 76:89). God is quick to give us large blessings for our small obedience! Geometrically, if little gears were to represent our obedience and large gears God's generous blessings for us all, as they do, we could grasp even further insights into God's character!

This generous pattern of intertwinings and blessings should fill us all with anticipation concerning the divine promise about how "eye hath not seen, nor ear heard, neither have entered into the heart of man, the things which God hath prepared for them that love him" (1 Corinthians 2:9). Such generosity is consistent, too, with the statement that, "I, the Lord, . . . delight to honor those who serve me in righteousness and in truth unto the end" (D&C 76:5). The word *delight* is much more than

God's routinely making good on a promise! *Delight* describes the feelings of a Perfect Father.

One other reason for my citing the foregoing and intertwining samples is to make a record of them for my and Colleen's posterity. These individuals see my weaknesses. Hence, for them, my wish parallels that of Moroni:

> Condemn me not because of mine imperfection, . . . but rather give thanks unto God that he hath made manifest unto you our imperfections, that ye may learn to be more wise than we have been (Mormon 9:31).

It will please me greatly if our children, their spouses, and their children, though imperfect, too, become "more wise than [I] have been."

God has been so generous to me! I, like Nephi, have a personal knowledge of His goodness. His longsuffering has provided me, again and again, with much-needed chances to improve—for which there has been *and still is* so much room!

Therefore, having already written and said so much in my ministry—perhaps too much, really—in the sunset of my service I identify with Jacob's words, "What can I say more?" (Jacob 6:12.) However, this small volume of "more" at least constitutes "One more strain of praise" ("Sing We Now at Parting," *Hymns*, no. 156).

Index